LOVE AMONG THE RUINS

LINDA AZÉMA

ISBN: 1-4033-9372-9 (Electronic)
ISBN: 1-4033-9373-7 (Softcover)

Library of Congress Control Number: 2002095703

This book is printed on acid free paper.

Printed in the United States of America
Bloomington, IN

Scripture is taken from the New American Standard Bible, Copyright 1960, 1962, 1963, 1968, 1971, 1972, 1973, 1975, 1977, 1995 by the Lockman Foundation. Used by permission.

For further information, or to pose any questions or express comments concerning this publication, please feel free to contact "Image Ministries" via email at www.imageministries.com

1stBooks - rev. 12/12/02

Acknowledgements

I would like to thank two people who spent many hours helping me to clarify the message of this book: Carolynn Spere and Linda Hamilton. Their faithfulness to the task and determination for excellence is deeply appreciated, and finishes by making this book so much better. When I struggled, they were always quick to remind me of their conviction that there is great need for the message and many will be encouraged through reading it. How amazing, that I should be blessed with such friends!

Contents

Chapter 1

When Life Isn't Fair

How much do we allow outside influences to affect us? The comments people make to me (or those I discover they have said about me), the actions of others (especially those actions I don't want to receive but which bombard me nonetheless), my own tendency to compare myself to the person I'm standing next to, and the reactions from others I encounter as I walk through the events and circumstances of my life—all these things shape how we see ourselves and work slowly over the years to convince us of who we are (and who we are not).

I remember when I was a little girl and received an invitation to my first party with my friends from school. They had a real swimming pool at their house! We were told to bring our swimsuits and we would be able to swim all afternoon if we felt like it! I had been swimming before with my brother and sisters and other kids from our little village, in the swimming hole of the stream that ran through our farm, and in lakes and rivers nearby. But now I had the chance to attend my very first party away from my family with just my own friends, and swim in a real swimming pool in their back yard!

In the midst of dunking each other off the plastic rafts, diving from the edge of the pool, and trying to be the one to make the biggest cannonball splash, one of my friends stopped to look at me and said, "Did you know that your ears stick straight out from the sides of your head?" No one had ever told me that before! I didn't know what to say. Little girls and boys often don't know what to say in moments like these, do they? (Big girls and boys often don't either.) But not long after that, I pretended I was tired of swimming and got out of the pool to find my towel and try my best to dry and fluff my hair so that it would cover my ears. It was years before the mention of a group swimming party didn't make me cringe inside.

When I was about eight years old, I was having such a great time swinging on the swings at the baseball park where my brother was playing in a game that I didn't take the time to notice the little boy swinging next to me. When I jumped off of my swing, his wooden swing slammed into the side of my head and down I went. I didn't pass out,

1

though. I was awake the whole time the doctor stitched up the ripped-open skin and heard him saying over and over how lucky I was that the swing had hit where it did. A half-inch further and I would have lost my eye.

I didn't feel so lucky when, a couple of years later, a girl at school said to me, "Don't you wish you could get rid of that ugly scar on your face?"

You can't imagine the amount of make-up that was smeared over that spot, trying to cover the blemish that eventually attracted the question a teenaged girl doesn't want to hear, "How did you get that scar on your face?"

When I was nineteen and facing the exciting prospect of spending a year of university study in France, I decided it would probably be a good idea to get my teeth checked before I went overseas (even though I hated dentists and hadn't been to one in years). I had no idea what might happen if I had a problem and needed to have a tooth repaired over there!

During the four return visits it took to finish all of the sixteen fillings that were needed, the dentist said, "It's a shame you weren't given proper dental treatment when you were younger. Those teeth of yours could have been corrected and they wouldn't be so crooked. But, it's too late; nothing can be done now. You'll just have to learn to live with it!" The pictures taken of me for a long time after that will show you proof that I was secretly trying to teach myself to smile without showing my teeth.

When I was about thirty-two years old, a family friend came to visit us while we were living in Iowa. It was fun to take him along with me, running errands and grocery shopping all over the area, while the kids were in school and my husband was at work. It was fun to watch him chat with the people in the small-town shops we visited and "talk country" with our friends the pig farmers and with the trapper who caught beaver and all sorts of wild animals.

But when we came home that day and were unloading the car, he stood back and looked at me as I reached over to pull another bag out of the trunk and said, "You sure do have a big butt! Yup, you sure got the hips, didn't you?" I never told anyone what had been said, but people were amazed how much weight I lost soon after that; and I found myself particularly attracted to shirts and tops that could be worn out over the waist and looked "slimming."

I grew up on a farm in Chester County, in southeastern Pennsylvania. It's now an elite residential area that could easily be mistaken for a suburb of Philadelphia. But when I was born there in 1950, it was just a sleepy, little, quiet village surrounded with wide-open dairy farmland. Ours was the only chicken farm. Thousands of chickens to care for meant there was lots of hard work every day. But after summer suppers, Dad would line the kids up outside and be the judge as we ran races. He would watch me race the others and say, "You run like a little deer!" And I pushed myself to outrun everybody, convinced I was going to be a great runner someday.

The only school in our area was a little two-room schoolhouse with first, second, and third grade on the first floor in one large room with one teacher. The fourth, fifth, and sixth grades were upstairs in the other room with another teacher. There weren't very many people living in our area so, from third grade on, I only had six children in my class. I received straight A's (the highest grade possible). I always knew the answers before the other students in my class and quickly finished my work, so I had plenty of time to listen while the teacher taught the older ones something I would have in my lessons the next year. It wasn't hard for me to be convinced that I was smarter than most.

When sixth grade ended, I was excited that I would be able to attend the "big" school next year: Junior High School! It was going to be a long bus-ride each day because it was further away in a bigger town called Downingtown, but I was thrilled that I would finally be in such a big, exciting place and compete with so many more kids.

It was bigger than I thought. I soon found it's one thing to be the smartest in a class of six, but now I was comparing my smartness to three hundred others in my seventh grade class! Arithmetic disappeared and became "Modern Math." Science class turned into "Biology." And worst of all, gym class entered my life and I discovered the mortifying experience of being required to undress and run through the showers in the middle of twenty-five other young girls, all in various stages of growth and awkward budding femaleness!

My mother played the piano. When I was about six years old, she was surprised to find me picking out the notes of the song she had played the night before. I had no music in front of me and had never played the piano before. I was quickly whisked off to a piano teacher for lessons, being told I had natural talent that was a gift. After four or five years of drudgery in lessons that bored me to death, my teacher wondered if I didn't want to give up piano because, as she put it, "You might be gifted, but you're too lazy to ever become an accomplished musician!"

In the middle of my senior year in high school, my father announced to me that I was going to college. When I was told I needed to choose a subject for my major in college, my French teacher was absolutely adamant that majoring in French would prove to be a disaster! "Linda," she finally exclaimed, "I have had you in my class for three years! You are horrible in French! You know nothing! You have been lazy through the whole experience, only doing as much work as you knew you needed to do at the end of each year so you could go on to the next level with the rest of your friends! You will never learn to speak French, let alone be capable of teaching it to anyone else!"

Why am I telling you about these memories? One of the first times I shared these stories from my past was at a retreat near Detroit, Michigan, where I was invited to be the speaker. At that time, we were living in England and I had flown from London to Detroit just days before the retreat began. Sounds glamorous? Anyone with very much international travel experience will tell you: overseas airline flights can be anything but glamorous, especially when flying in the economy section with other mere mortals such as I!

When I finished sharing these same personal stories you've just read, I looked out over the audience at that retreat and asked, "Did I come four thousand miles, willing to cram my body into that wonderful space we call an economy section airline seat, and then sit there for the next nine hours wondering how I will ever straighten my knees again, trying to ignore the body odor of the person sitting two seats away (so hoping he won't lift both arms into the air for a big, long stretch one more time), while I eat what they call 'dinner' and I feel can only be called 'airplane food,' making every attempt not to glare at the woman who insists on standing in the aisle to chat with her friends during the movie right in line with my view of the screen…

…then force my body to maneuver a 360-degree turn and sit down, once I've locked myself into the even tinier space they call 'a lavatory' because I can't hold back the urge I was so hoping I could repress until we landed, just as the loud speaker over my head crackles and hisses out the captain's voice, 'Ladies and gentlemen we are experiencing a bit of turbulence. Please return to your seats and fasten your seatbelts.'"

4

"Did I do all that," I asked that group in Michigan, "and come here because I needed to share these little-known things about myself hoping you'd feel sorry for me?"

No, of course not. Using some stories from my own past, I was trying to remind us how much we allow outside influences to affect us. The things people say, the things people do, the way we tend to compare ourselves with those around us, and the reactions we encounter, all work together to shape how we see ourselves. Gradually, over the years, often without us being particularly aware that it's happening, these things may work slowly to distort our view of who we are (and perhaps wrongly convince us of who we are not). Isn't this true? Do you agree with me?

Testing the crowd climate in Michigan to see if my audience was identifying with me, I asked them, "How many of you have had similar experiences—both positive, affirming experiences that built you up and negative, derogatory ones that tore away at your self-confidence? Raise your hand, if your answer is yes." Then I told them to keep their hands raised and turn to look around them. It was a significant moment. Every person in the room was raising a hand.

When I gave an opportunity for volunteers to stand and briefly share one of their own experiences, it was striking how poignant their stories were. It was also obvious how much emotion was still attached to the memory that was shared, even though many spoke of events that had occurred several years ago. Some stories even bordered on being humorous until you caught the distant look of pain that momentarily rushed to the surface in the person's eyes just before she sat back down again.

One woman spoke of being told she would never be able to sing properly because she had such a horrible voice. When she was a child, she was told not to sing so loudly when her family was in church because it bothered other people who were trying to worship. People have told us about being openly ridiculed and criticized by parents who compared them to a brother or sister who was obviously Dad or Mom's favorite. We've heard stories about spouses being verbally abusive, putting their partners in awkward and embarrassing positions, both in private and in front of other family members and friends.

I could continue with the list but, as you can already see, few (if any) positive or affirming stories are mentioned. And each time I listen, I have no trouble identifying the hurt, deception, and disappointment.

The marks and scars still cause tremors in the voice and tears in the eyes, however subtle and controlled by a person who tries hard to believe it's all just a memory now. Is it? Are we willing to admit the power those memories may still have?

You see, now I can afford to get my hair styled and use just the right invisible product on it that holds the style and you don't notice my ears, and I can practice until I'm able to stand in front of you capable of ignoring the scar on my face, and I can plan my smiles to look natural even though only a part of my teeth are showing, and I can diet and re-diet and exercise until my hips are trimmed, and I can earn the university diploma that proves how smart I am, and I can replace my high school French teacher (which I did, while she took a sabbatical leave) and teach in the same classroom where she told me I would never learn to speak French, and I can work for nine years to write and rewrite my first book four times, proving that I'm not lazy...

...and underneath it all, I can still see myself as a little girl from some small, backwoods, country village with ears that stick straight out from the side of my head, and crooked teeth, and a huge, ugly scar right next to my left eye that everybody's looking at every time they talk to me, and a fat butt, who's smart as heck and isn't it a shame she has such lofty ideas because as lazy as she is, she'll never accomplish half the things she sets out to do in life!

Do you have leftover images from your past that affect how you see yourself, too? Is it possible that as hard as we work to improve the impression we make—whether we do it because we call ourselves "Christians" and want to measure up, or whether we do it because we just want to be accepted as "a good person"—inside, we still secretly hear the same old messages playing and replaying through our minds? Why is this a struggle? Why does it sometimes seem like there's an internal, private war going on in our minds? This might surprise you.

God is not unaware of the damage other people can do to us. He knows every detail of the damage that has been done to you.

"So what is He doing about it?" you may feel like asking (the power of your question hinting at the existence of anxiety, doubts and fears you most often seek to hide). What is God doing? What has He done? What does He intend to do? MUCH. Most often, more than many men and women realize or grasp, though we occasionally catch glimpses of "something beyond" seeping through the cracks in the walls we've built surrounding the house we call *belief.*

"Thinking it Through"
(Optional Personal Application)

Suggestion: Find a piece of paper and write a letter. Address it to God, if you feel you can accept the possibility of communicating your most personal thoughts to Him at this time in your life. If not, don't address it to anyone. Just write for the sake of expressing your feelings in a tangible manner.

To help you get started, read each phrase below and decide how you would finish the sentence. But most importantly, be honest with yourself! Don't struggle to compose something pretty, poetic, or godly-sounding, or spiritual. Just be real! Take a blank piece of paper and write down your true feelings without polishing them.

* [p.s. It's okay to admit it if the word *unfair* comes to mind.]

"I know I should accept who I am and not be so concerned about my physical appearance and how smart I am, but _____

_____

_____

_____

_____

_____

_____!"

"I wish I could erase some parts of my past, especially _____

_____

_____

_____

_____

_____

_____!"

"When I look at my life and the image I have of myself, this is what I see and this is how I feel: _____

_____

_____

_____

_____

_____

_____!"

Suggestion: When you finish thinking through those thoughts, consider saying the following verse from the Bible aloud, personalizing it this way. This is a promise from God that He will respond to the things you've written in your letter, if you're willing to admit you would like things to change.

"[I] will call, and the LORD will answer; [I] will cry, and He will say, 'Here I am.'...[My] light will rise in the darkness, and [the gloom of my life] will become like midday" (Isaiah 58: 9,10).

Suggestion: There was a KEY principle highlighted in this chapter. Though you may feel terribly alone and isolated in the situations of life you're facing (and may doubt the existence of God or find it hard to believe He cares about what happens to you), I challenge you to read that key principle aloud once again. No matter how much of it you presently believe, are you willing to investigate this concept further with me?

God is not unaware of the damage other people can do to us. He knows every detail of the damage that has been done to me.

Chapter 2

When The World Is In Charge

"Does anybody really love me?" This is the question my husband and I have heard so often. Speaking publicly and teaching seminars about marriage, parenting, dealing with past mistakes, resolving conflicts, personal finances, career strategies and work ethics, leadership training, and effective small group dynamics almost always leads people to come to us after a conference for private advice and counsel. We listen to their stories.

While we were living in England, we also became involved in a new work that was supported by the church we attended there. It provides a place for those who need private, individual counseling in a difficult situation they are facing, and it is called "The Family Support Centre." Over the span of several months, we had the opportunity to train many of the counselors at the center. Not long after they opened to the public, word spread throughout the area that help was available and they began facing more complicated cases than they had expected.

My husband and I were asked to help some of the counselors and sit with them in sessions with their clients. Once again, we found ourselves listening as people opened their hearts before us. The details of their stories varied. But each contained the harsh elements of disappointment, deception, desertion, and destruction that led to a final question. Worded differently, expressed in terms that fit each particular story, there was the same underlying, heart-rending question.

It's the same question which is asked when people come to us after the public conferences I mentioned earlier. Finishing his or her story, the person looks at us with eyes that beg for a deep, lasting touch of reassurance—sometimes tear-filled eyes, sometimes dry-eyed, tears spent—and asks, "Does *anybody* love me? Really love me? Love me for who I am, not for what they want me to be, or expect me to be, or wish I was? Is there anybody I can really count on, or rely upon and depend on?"

At the end of the last chapter, I said, "God is not unaware of the damage other people can do to us." I see evidence in the Bible that confirms this. I find this evidence in the life stories we can read there. I call people whose experiences are described in the Bible, "Bible people." Why do I do that? Because we've done it for years, most of us who have some knowledge of the stories about people like Abraham, Moses, Jacob, Joseph, David, Solomon, Matthew, Mark, Luke, John, and Paul. We say the names of Bible characters such as these, and immediately we've moved over a mental slot or two, out of our realm of reality, and into the "utterly-holy" realm in which we've become convinced they lived.

We walked away from story time in our children's church class with perhaps a subconscious impression that these people were wonderful, holier-than-thou, godly people who lived a protected life and walked around surrounded by the blessings of Almighty God. Little wonder, as adults, so many of us ultimately reject the possibility that those stories could have any bearing on the situations we face today, or that a look at the life of one of these characters from the Bible could help us. There's no comparison! There's no common ground! They could never have dealt with the things we face today! They were "Bible people!" (Now you can see why I call them that.)

Well, listen to what one "Bible person" named David said about how life was going when he wrote Psalm 56:

"Be gracious, O God, for man has trampled upon me; fighting all day long, he oppresses me. My foes have trampled upon me all day long, for they are many who fight proudly against me...All day long they distort my words; all their thoughts are against me for evil. They attack, they lurk. They watch my steps, as they have waited to take my life" (verse 1,2,5,6).

Just sounds like he was having loads of fun, doesn't it? By the way, a more literal translation of the phrase in verse 1, *"man has trampled me..."* would be, "man has SNAPPED at me..." Now is it beginning to sound like you could relate to this Bible person? Okay, back to the Bible. Same guy, one chapter later:

"My soul is among lions; I must lie among those who breathe forth fire, even the sons of men, whose teeth are spears and arrows, and their tongue a sharp sword" (Psalm 57:4). Tell me you haven't had to deal with at least one person in your life whose words could pretty well be described like this! You know what it's like to hear words hurled at you like spears and angry darting arrows meant to pierce the skin, with a tongue pointed and sharpened like a sword poised to stab you in the heart, don't you?

Hold on, my friend. The worst is yet to come. How many of us have had this experience? *"Even my close friend, in whom I trusted, who ate my bread, has lifted up his heel against me"* (Psalm 41:9).

Have you ever encountered someone doing these things, perhaps for the first time unmasking a cold, hard heart? David, this "Bible person" did. He begs God, *"Keep me as the apple of the eye; hide me in the shadow of Thy wings…"* [Why? What's he hiding from?] *"…from the wicked who despoil me, my deadly enemies, who surround me. They have closed their unfeeling heart; with their mouth they speak proudly. They have now surrounded us in our steps; they set their eyes to cast us down to the ground. He is like a lion that is eager to tear, and as a young lion lurking in hiding places"* (Psalm 17: 8-12).

Does this sound like a war is going on, sound like some of the battles you've endured, some of the ways you've been attacked in the past? What a struggle we can go through, and people around us might not even realize what we're dealing with, or that they might be one of the persons contributing to our suffering! All the damage that can be done by the world around us! Why does it happen? I'll tell you why.

I've said God is not unaware of the things people do to you or say to you (or say about you). But God is not the only one who is aware of you. There are ugly, selfish people who will use you in their own designs, aren't there? The world is also capable of working in the hands of an evil one, the devil who is called Satan. He is the enemy of God. Satan hates God and anything or anybody in any way connected with God.

Satan knows he cannot touch your spirit or your soul. If you are a Christian, you believe Jesus Christ is the Son of God. You have asked God to forgive you on the basis of your belief that Jesus Christ died on the cross to pay the penalty for your sin, and you have returned to embrace God as your Father. Satan knows you belong to God and he cannot undo that. Your spirit is forever in union with God's Spirit.

If you are not a Christian, Satan still cannot touch your soul. The Bible tells us we were each created in the image of God. Figuratively, you can think of it this way: the fingerprint of God has left its trace upon each of us as we were shaped and formed in our mother's womb. Satan takes one look at you, recognizes that fingerprint traced across your spirit, and knows he can't touch that.

The world can't touch your spirit or your soul. Satan can't touch your spirit or your soul. So the world and Satan will attack what they can touch: your body and your mind. Satan cannot alter the way you view your soul. But he can alter the way you view your body and how smart or intelligent you think you are. And so, my friend, early in our lives the world and Satan begin their horrible work in these two domains of personal perception—working to distract us with obsessions about how we look physically and how we perform intellectually—as we constantly compare ourselves with others, until these thoughts swallow up all of our time and energy.

Build the body, build up the stores of knowledge in education of all sorts, concentrate on my body and my brain, and Satan knows there will be little time or energy left to consider my spirit and my soul in pursuit of the things of God.

If you are a Christian, Satan hates your body. Did you know that? Satan hates your body and your mind because you have made it the throne of the Most High God, the Holy One.

If you are not a Christian, whether you believe Satan exists or not doesn't really matter. You may not even be willing to believe that God exists. That doesn't matter in this case, either. Satan still hates your body and your mind because they were created by God (in the image of God); and remember…Satan hates God.

In both cases, the devil's agenda is to destroy your body and mind which is meant to be God's dwelling place and throne, or at least to make you believe it's an ugly throne, not nearly as attractive and intelligent as someone else's throne!

You don't like your body? Satan knows exactly why God has made you the way He has. Satan knows, but doesn't want you to realize or remember that God only made your body to be the frame around the picture. Maybe you've heard this before. Think about it. What is a frame meant to do when you look at a picture? Enhance the picture! Simply attract your attention to the picture itself! The artist, the creator really wants you to see the picture, not the frame!

Let me ask you a question. How often do you suppose people go to art museums and art galleries because they want to see some beautiful frames they've never seen before? You can see my point. They go there because they're looking for beauty in the pictures and hardly even notice the frame!

I suggest to you, if we are living and thinking the way God desires, the way we were created to live and think, we will search for a friend or someone to love (and we, too, will want to be loved) by looking for beauty in the picture. The frame may originally attract us or distract us.

But given the chance, it is the discovery of what the frame surrounds that eventually captures our hearts and draws us together. And amazingly enough, when that happens, the frame seems to attract our attention less and less! Why? Because of what we have found deep inside the picture! From this new perspective, we realize the frame the Master Artist designed fulfills and completes the picture. Nothing else would do around the edge, once we truly know and love the middle!

So what does Satan do about this? He doesn't want people looking for beauty deep inside the picture (the person). He hates what's there (our spirits and our souls) because that's where God's throne is, or where it isn't but could be. He doesn't want people to consider how empty they are inside or contemplate the true state of their hearts. So he tries to get everyone to focus on the external, instead!

And what do we end up with? A world full of people spending all their time, energy and money to work on being a person that looks better and appears smarter than (or at least as good as) everyone else! Think of all the different sources the world uses to direct your thoughts towards your body and your mind—clothing, cosmetics, hairstyles, diet programs, physical fitness and health clubs, exercise videos, sports and athletic competitions, and advertisements for everything from toothpaste to the car you drive are all focused on how you look. How many books, videos, self-help training courses, night classes, college programs and academic or how-to technology degrees will it take to convince you that you're as smart as the next person?

Please don't misunderstand me. There's nothing wrong with the care we take in personal hygiene or the choice of clothing we wear. And I have great respect for those who continue their education. My point is not that we *shouldn't* do those things. I'm more concerned with why we're doing them. And in that light, I have another question that will make my perspective clearer. How much time do you and I spend concerning ourselves with the frame, while we neglect the picture in the middle? How much time do you and I spend being obsessed with the body and the mind, while we neglect the spirit and the soul?

You might be thinking, "Yes, but we still need to take care of our bodies so that we're healthy." I agree. I'm not suggesting a total disregard that would end in neglect of my physical condition or mental health. Instead, I'm suggesting the need for balance and possibly a realignment of some priorities in our lives.

Being very sick for nearly two years (which included a struggle against E-coli bacteria) helped me to realize how much more important good health is than good looks. Now I have a whole new respect and appreciation for being able to do simple things, and doing them without pain or sickness. I know we are to be good stewards of these bodies God has fashioned for us. I don't deny my responsibility to be careful of what I eat and consider how it's going to affect my system, either to nourish me or to harm me. I don't deny my responsibility to be knowledgeable about how my body functions and use good judgment in what I do, or do not do, with my body.

But once I've done all those things, how do I deal with the way I feel about my body? How do you deal with it? What do I do when I look in the mirror and realize I'm not content with what I see, the things I wish were different? What happens in your mind when you look in your mirror? How we answer these questions (or if we choose to ignore them) can be very revealing, my friend. If we're honest, most of us will admit we have a struggle somewhere in this private realm of dealing with our physical bodies.

My greatest struggle of acceptance in this area is not that I wish I were slimmer or sleeker or prettier. My complaint has always been that I wish I were stronger and didn't get sick so often. Ask my husband the number of times he's heard me say, "I wish I were strong like you."

In that light, I have a message for anyone who may also be dealing with sickness, especially chronic sickness—sickness you cannot simply cure, or take medication and be restored to normal health. I suffer from constant muscle pain, some days worse than others. I'm learning to apply a thought God finally got through my thick head while I was sick for those two years I mentioned earlier. It has to do with sickness or pain or disability, but we can also apply it to this idea of simply accepting what we see when we look in the mirror and what we believe others see when they look at us out there in the world. So, it's really a message for all of us. Here's what God made clear to me:

I will have all eternity to praise God and demonstrate His tremendous love and faithfulness to me when I get to heaven and I am given a new and perfect body.

I only have this short time while I live here on this earth to praise God and demonstrate that I believe in His tremendous love and faithfulness to me with this less-than-perfect body, demonstrating to

15

myself and to all others around me that I trust God's perfect plan for me when He made my body just like it is!

There it is. It's only a beginning. I invite you to apply this perspective as you consider life in the midst of your physical difficulties. Think on this thought and apply it to yourself in your own spirit for a while, every day for weeks and months, and see what happens to your attitudes and your long-term outlook on life. It has changed mine.

Now, let's go back to the world full of people spending their time, energy, and money to work on having a frame that looks better than, and appears smarter than, (or at least as good as) everyone else's. Back to our questions:

How much time do you and I spend concerning ourselves with the body and the mind, and neglect the soul and the spirit?

How often do I get upset, hung up, side-tracked, depressed or disgusted with myself because of the images the world has loaded into my mind telling me how they see me? And, what do I do about it?

It certainly will do no good to feel guilty now that this is clearer to us. That would only allow Satan a different sort of victory with us living in the doldrums or in "the depths of despair," as Anne of Green Gables would put it! Let's remember that I said God is aware of how the world has affected you. And now, to that thought, I add this:

God is not only aware of how the world has affected you. He also has an agenda for how He wants to help you and heal your damaged heart.

God wants to repair your heart.
God wants to rebuild your heart.
And finally, God wants to refill your heart.

"Thinking it through"
(Optional Personal Application)

Suggestion: Find a Bible and look up these verses from the chapter you just read. Read them again and think about how they might describe things in your own life (now, in the past, or what the future looks like stretching in front of you). It might be enlightening to write down thoughts as they come to mind.

Psalm 56: 1,2,5,6
"In the past, _____
_____."

"Now, _____
_____."

"The future _____
_____."

Psalm 57:4
"In the past, _____
_____."

"Now, _____
_____."

"The future _____
_____."

Psalm 41:9
"In the past, _____
_____."

"Now, _____

_____ ."

"The future _____
_____,"

Psalm 17: 8-12

"In the past, _____
_____."

"Now, _____
_____."

"The future _____
_____."

Suggestion: Write down how you would honestly finish these thoughts.

"When I take a look at where my life is right now, I feel like _____
_____!"

"Things would be a whole lot easier and less complicated, if it weren't for _____
_____!"

"Where is my life headed? I wonder if I will ever _____
_____!"

Suggestion: We've added a bit to the KEY principle you read in chapter one. Read it again and, by personalizing it, consider how accepting that this is true could impact your life today.

God is not only aware of how the world has affected me. He also has an agenda for how He wants to help me and heal my damaged heart.

Chapter 3

When You Wish You Could Forget

God is the Creator and Designer who made you. But do you see yourself as His creation? Can you see yourself from His perspective? Have you lost sight of who you are meant to be, what you are created to be, how you are designed and fashioned to portray one unique message to the world? We've talked about the damage the world and Satan have done to distort how we see ourselves, getting us so upset, hung up, side-tracked, depressed or disgusted about what we think we look like that we spend all of our time working to improve the way our bodies look and how smart we appear to others.

Remember, we said Satan hates our bodies and minds. If you're a Christian, your body and mind is a place where Jesus Christ reigns as Lord. If you're not a Christian, your body and mind is still the place where Jesus might reign someday, should you decide to open your heart and allow God to enter and comfort you. What did we say Satan does to distract our attention so that we have no energy or time left to give any attention to our hearts (the middle of the picture)? Satan gets us to focus on the frame!

You can eventually be deeply damaged inside your heart and mind as a result of the things the world and Satan have done to you over the years. They ripped and slashed at their view of your frame, telling you and showing you how your body and mind appear to them, pointing out the parts that don't measure up to what they think you could be, or should be. You might be hiding it from others, but you're painfully aware of the wounds and scars, aren't you?

God wants time with you to repair the damage the world and Satan have done by distorting the image you have of your "frame." First, He must be allowed time to reveal the distortions and repair the image, in order for you to realize who He created you to be and how He sees you. But in order to do that, God needs to touch your heart.

Uh-oh! Now we could be in trouble! I can hear thoughts rumbling through the mind of some readers: "Houston, we have a problem! Large imposing object approaching the ship! Request permission to close down all the hatches and either blow it to bits or bail out!"

I can imagine you thinking, "Whoa! Now why did you have to go straight to the heart-thing? I'm not sure I want God messing with my heart! This is big-time stuff! How do I know I can trust Him? I've opened myself up to others before and look what they did to me! Now you're talking about me opening myself up to God? I'm not sure I'm ready to do that! What's He going do to me, anyway? You know, I haven't necessarily been all that good all the time and I've heard He's this holy God and everything, so maybe He doesn't really like me. You say He's my Father and all that. Well, that's just it. I've had plenty of what my father did when he didn't like what I'd been doing, so I'm not really interested in more of that sort of stuff, if you know what I mean!"

Yes, He wants to be your Father; and yes, He wants you to open your heart so He can touch it. How do you know you can trust Him? Well, maybe going back to our analogy will help. Let's remember we've been saying that our struggles come from the world and Satan causing us to focus on the frame. Now I would like you to consider an actual framed painting hanging in an art gallery. Who painted the picture? An artist. A master artist and designer.

But suppose a thief broke into the art gallery and mutilated and damaged the frame of that picture. The frame is destroyed. Yet, somehow, the thief's knife slashed away at the frame but never touched the picture itself. How do you think the artist who painted the picture will feel when he sees what the thief has done? Upset, but glad the picture he worked so hard to design is still undamaged and intact. What does he do? He replaces or restores the frame.

Now suppose another thief breaks in and attacks the same piece of art. But this time he slashes the picture too, not just the frame. How do you think the artist will react this time? Can you imagine his grief? Can you envision the disappointment and sadness that will be on his face when he enters and sees his work destroyed? The owner of the gallery who bought the picture might be upset, too. But do you think anyone else could possibly be as upset as the artist who created the picture?

He might even be angry. Sure, he can paint another picture. He can even try to duplicate the one that was destroyed. But, he knows it will never be exactly the same again. The moment of creation will be different. The need will be different. That work of art was created with a special message in mind. No other work, even done by the same artist, will ever capture the exact moment, the exact message, the exact meaning this one piece was designed to speak to the world.

I assure you, I am absolutely convinced God feels exactly this same way about each of us! Don't ask me to prove to you that God is the One who created us, and that it isn't just a biological process of sexual intercourse, conception, and cell multiplication that eventually works together to form a baby. The Bible starts with God's Hand at work forming the first man and woman. And hundreds of years later that same Bible-person David said, *"You have formed my inward parts, O God! You did weave me together inside my mother's womb"* (Psalm 139:13).

I know those words from the Bible are true. They are not just David's emotions rushing to the surface and erupting in some poetic way to describe the beginning of his existence. I know without a doubt in my mind that those words perfectly describe the actual motions of God at work forming a baby inside a woman's womb. He is the Creator! He is the Artist! I know, because I'm the thief who broke in and destroyed one of His works! I aborted the baby He was creating inside of me! I felt His anger! I heard the sorrow in His voice!

Didn't you sense yourself agreeing with me in the illustration of a thief breaking into an art gallery and damaging a precious painting? Didn't you agree that no one would be as grieved by the criminal act as the one who painted the picture? Likewise, my friend, I know by personal experience, only the Artist, only the Creator would get that upset about what I did! And only the Artist, only the Creator would have the right and the power to forgive me and not leave me to rot in the self-made prison of my guilt, but release me and love me, instead!

God is the Creator and Designer who made you. It doesn't matter where you've come from or who you've been or what you've been doing. No one cares about you like He does. No one values you as much as He does. No one understands you so completely as does God. No one will ever touch your heart with more tenderness and care and love than He will. I'm asking you to consider allowing Him to do that. God wants to touch your heart. God wants to repair the damage that has been done. You know there has been damage. We've all experienced moments of life that have damaged our hearts. We are all in need of repair. As I said before, you might be hiding it from others, but you are painfully aware of the rips and tears—the scars—in the middle of the picture, aren't you?

The scars are on your heart. The scars on your heart are distorting the way you see yourself and affect the way you can respond to people around you, whether accepting their love or enduring their abuse. The first step in God's plan to repair your heart is a step you must take. Why?

God cannot do (in your heart) what you do not give Him permission to do, because God WON'T do what you do not WANT Him to do.

God will wait until you step toward Him and open your heart to let Him touch it. (Ah! This may be a new thought to some of you, already revealing one of the many ways the world and Satan have not only distorted our self image, but have also succeeded in distorting our view of who God is and what is the character of His work in us.)

At the end of this chapter, you will find some suggestions to guide you in a personal application of the material you're reading here. We've been duped into focusing on the frame. God wants to pivot our perspective from focusing on ourselves, and help us learn to focus on Him instead. I hope you will take the time either alone, with a friend, or with a group of friends to read the thoughts at the end of the chapter. Make an effort to search for an answer that will be a deeply honest response to the questions that are asked. Stretch yourself to pray the prayers that are suggested.

This is the first part of the process God will use to pivot your perspective. Whether you do it for the very first time, or as a reminder and rededication, I pray that you are willing (in the midst of whatever circumstance of life you may presently be facing) to reconsider your belief that God is the Creator and Designer of your very being, every part of you. For some, it won't take long. For others, it might turn out to be one of those "all-nighters," stretching into the wee hours of the morning.

To each of you, I promise this: allow yourself the freedom to return to God, acknowledging that He is your Creator and Designer, and you will find God the Revealer and Comforter coming to meet you. When we're willing to put forth this kind of effort, we have the wonderful possibility of knowing God Himself! This is what happens when knowing and hearing and reading about God, turns into surrender to God.

The same thing happened to another Bible-person named Job who, finally coming to the end of his long struggle, exclaimed, *"God, I have heard of you by the hearing of the ear; but now my eye sees you"* (Job 42:5). God will reveal Himself. He promises to do that when we genuinely and sincerely seek Him. *"You will seek Me and find Me, when you search for Me with all your heart"* (Jeremiah 29:13).

So why don't we do it? Why do we hold back? (Some of you will, you know. Perhaps you can already feel yourself doing it.) If we can be so assured that God will answer, why don't we pray these prayers more readily? Because we're not so sure that the only thing God is going to reveal...is Him! Faced with an opportunity for this kind of prayer-encounter with God, some of us can take a quick look at our pasts (all the way up to yesterday) and say, "Hey! Sure! I've heard about this Omniscient, all-knowing God before! I know what He'll reveal if I go to Him!"

I've been trying to present a description of God's character and His will toward us by saying He desires to be known as Father-God, the Creator, Designer, Revealer, and Comforter. Sounds great for others, but you might be sitting there secretly thinking to yourself, "Right! You expect me to believe that? Even better, you expect me to like that? Look at who I am! Who would be thankful for the body and mind I've got? Look at my life! Why would God love ME with the past I've got piled up behind me? You ask me to take all that to God, and all I see is a cranky Creator who by now probably realizes He created a Designer disaster! And when He takes a look at my past, the Revealer is going to turn into the Squealer because He'll blow the whistle on everything I've ever done and line up all my mistakes! Now, do you still think I'm going to feel like I've just met the Comforter?"

No wonder you don't want to pray! Do you see how distorted our view of God can be? Our own self-image is not the only thing the world and Satan have managed to damage. For many people, mention God, and the first image that pops into their minds is what? The Judge!

Yes, within the realms of God's justice, sin must be judged. Yes, God is Judge—the only wise, unbiased, unchanging Judge. You can count on it. You can count on Him...hating evil and despising sin because He knows (far more than we know) how it hurts us, the ones the Master Artist loves. Sin damages and destroys what He has created us to be. It damages the message He has planned for us to convey while we live here in this world among other men, women, and children. Yes, you can count on it. When you come before God, the sins of your past come right into the picture with you.

But this may surprise you. Unlike the picture of men and women we have encountered who have attempted to judge us here on this earth, God the Judge is not eager to judge us. You might imagine Him sitting on His Throne in heaven and catching a glimpse of you coming towards Him. But as soon as He notices it's you, He jumps up from His seat, squares His arms tightly across His chest, leans back with a stern look in His eyes and says, "So! It's finally you! I've been waiting for this one! It sure took you long enough!"

No, as a matter of fact, everyone I know who has set out to find God met someone else first. Thinking the journey had just begun (and that it would take a long time because they'd have to work very hard to get there), as they approached the Throne of heaven, someone else came to meet them—someone called the Mediator, the Savior. Someone named Jesus Christ stepped forward and stood between the person and Father-God.

Why? Didn't Jesus want that person to meet God? Was He barring the way because the sinful past dragging along behind her was too dirty and disgusting to permit this person to appear before Holy God? No. He did indeed notice the sinful past she was carrying. And it made Him weep.

As He stepped forward, His eyes looked deeply into her eyes and He saw her heart, and wept at the pain the scars were causing her. As His hand touched her face to wipe away the tears, she felt some strange bumps and turned her head to get a closer look. Only then did she notice the scars on His hands and hear Him say, "I know. I have felt the pain that scars. You don't need to carry that load any more. I can take it from you. Give it to me. Father-God wants you to be free from it."

"He sees how it harms you, so He sent me to break the chains that have been wrapped around you, and rid you of your burden. I know you don't want to give it to Me because you're so sorry and ashamed that you brought all that with you, and you feel like you ought to deal with it yourself and not just pass your burdens to someone else. But this is why I died on the cross. You don't have the key to unlock the chains. I do." And He held up a very old, anciently old key, a key that looked like it had been around for a long time—times beyond her time—since the beginning of time.

He continued softly, so softly…gently soothing away her fears with His voice. "When I died on the cross, our enemy Satan did not kill me.

24

With his devious, deceitful lies he may have been tricking you to believe he did kill me and that was the end of my life. But he knows where I got this key, and when I got it."

"Holy Spirit and Father-God breathed life back into My body as I lay in the grave, and I rose up from that tomb, went straight through the gates of hell, walked past Satan and all his demons, tilted up that little high-chair he tries to pretend is a throne, and took out from under it the key I'm holding in My Hand—the only Hand that will ever have permission to touch this key—the only Hand that will ever have power to use this key—the only key that can ever unlock your chains and set you free..."

And suddenly His voice changed, only slightly, but she noticed the difference. "...*because MINE was the Hand that I nailed to the cross which Satan had prepared for you!*" She hadn't realized that her eyes had closed while Jesus was talking, but at the sound of this new voice, her eyes flew open! It couldn't be! She had to be sure! It was!

Jesus proclaiming, "*MINE was the Hand...*"
Father-God declaring, "*...that I nailed to the cross...*"
Holy Spirit revealing truth, "*...which Satan had prepared for you!*"

All three together, all three at once, and yet she heard each one separately at the same time! She could tell by His voice and see on His face Father-God's yearning to be reunited with one He had formed, and hold her in His arms. She could tell by His voice that Holy Spirit longed to comfort her and carry her deeper into the realm of Father-God.

"Let Me touch you and unlock those chains that hold you bound to your past," the voice of Jesus whispered one more time.

"But what will You do with my heart? What will happen to my life if I do that?" she pleaded. "And even if I let You do that—afterwards, won't it be the same thing all over again? When I go back out there into the world, won't people do those things to me again? Won't I be hurt and won't there be trouble anyway? Won't it just start all over again?"

For the briefest instant she thought she saw a flicker of anger streak through Jesus' eyes and the slightest hint of a growl rumble deep in His chest. Somehow in this moment when all things were becoming clear, she also knew His anger was not directed at her, but towards the evil one, Satan, who engraves his lies deeply upon the heart of each person he can touch, entangling them in his web of doubt and destruction, still working its horrible magic to keep another prisoner in his grip.

"You must trust Me that once you willingly allow Me to free you, no one can ever bind you up in those chains again! I will remove all that is evil and sinful from your past. It will be gone forever. I will cleanse you from every smudge and smear, and you will be completely clean. There is more…" and as He said that, it seemed His eyes looked far past her moment, deep into times, "…but will you trust Me for this much now?" she heard Him ask.

"Thinking it through"
(Optional Personal Application)

Suggestion: Read Matthew 7:7 in your Bible and answer these questions. Be careful not to answer too quickly. THINK about the implications of your answer!

Who does the knocking? _____

Who opens the door? _____

Who does the asking? _____

Who gives? _____

Who does the seeking? _____

Who finds? _____

Think of it this way: "Seek, and you **shall be found!**" Does that help?

Could it be that I've been working hard for so long on everything else in my life (making it all happen!) that when it comes to getting close to God, I think I've got to be the one to make that happen, too?

Am I so busy orchestrating my life that I've forgotten to wait and look for what **GOD** will do?

Suggestion: There was a KEY principle in the middle of this chapter. Take a look at it again. Read it aloud to yourself, personalizing it this way.

God cannot do (in my heart) what I do not give Him permission to do, because God WON'T do what I do not WANT Him to do.

God will wait until you step toward him and open your heart to let Him touch it. Have you ever done that? Are you willing to do that now? Or have you allowed God to touch your heart in the past, but there are new areas in your life since then that you've either been hiding from His view or ignoring when the light of His Word shines there and reveals? Apply the thoughts from Matthew 7:7.

"God will _____, but only when I _____."

(Will you?)

Chapter 4

When Your Eyes See Only Darkness

God loves you. God cares about you. God is the Master Artist who created and designed you. No one cares about you like He does. No one values you as much as He does. No one understands you like He does. No one will ever touch your heart with more tenderness and gentle, loving care than He will. God desires to demonstrate His love to you right now, right in the midst of your present life circumstances. And He knows what those circumstances are. God is intimately aware of every detail of your life.

"So what's He doing about it?" you may ask! Great things, but you may have become so distracted by the things of this world and Satan's tactics to discourage and destroy you that you're missing the moments when God wishes to demonstrate His glory in your life.

It might not seem like it to you, but I tell you God is real! God is alive! God is powerful and almighty! No matter how overwhelming your present life circumstance may appear, this God of whom the Bible speaks—the One True God—this God whom I love and serve is greater than your biggest problem! He is ABLE to meet your need! God's power stretches beyond the forces of even the mightiest world governments, beyond the demands of any social or economic system, beyond the so-called "laws" of medical, physical and mathematical science! His power breaks through the barriers we mere humans erect when we cry, "Impossible! Unbelievable! Incredible! Outrageous! Unrealistic!"

Considered alone—without the tempering force of love and care and affection—such power would be frightening, wouldn't it? But here is the good news, my friend. This same God of awe-inspiring power and strength and might is the One who loves you and me. How do I know? When I was 19 years old, I discovered words He has written to assure you and me of His intense desire to love us. God Almighty, the God of the universe says, *"I will welcome you. And I will be a Father to you, and you shall be sons and daughters to Me…"* (II Corinthians 6:17,18).

In fact, God goes so far in trying to help us understand how He wants to love us that He tells us, once we become His sons and daughters (Christians), we can cry out to Him, *"Abba!"* (Romans 8:15). Do you know what "Abba" means? It means, "Daddy," or "Papa," or "Pa," or whatever term your family uses as its affectionate expression for the father. Oh, my friend, since I became a Christian over 30 years ago, such things have happened in my life to strengthen my knowledge of God and build my trust in Him that when others ask me how I can be so strong, I can only say, "If you knew my Daddy…!"

Do we choose to believe in God when we're faced with overwhelming circumstances in our lives? Do we choose to turn to Him and seek His help? Or do we listen to what the world says "makes sense" and back down from our stand of faith in the face of the doubts and fears Satan whispers in our ears: "That's impossible! You're a fool! Do you know how people are going to mock you and make fun of you? Don't you realize who you are? You're nobody! Why would anyone listen to you? Why would God answer you? What makes you think you can do great things? You have no power! You have no authority! No one will follow you, and they won't believe it if you tell them you're making this choice because God has spoken to you!"

My husband Dominique is a French citizen. We were married in the United States and lived there for four years before moving back to France. When our son, Kacha (pronounced "Kasha") was born with a slightly deformed leg, the doctors in America told us, "No problem. We see this occasionally and it usually straightens out when the child begins to walk. Just wait."

When we moved back to France, Dominique's parents were not so reassuring. They finally convinced us to see a specialist whom they knew. By that time, Kacha was about 18 months old and walking; but the deformity of his right leg had not improved. His foot turned inward (nearly at a right angle to the other one) and his leg curved severely inward from the knee down to his ankle. The French doctor told us, since the American doctors had not even taken x-rays, they would have to do tests and then wait a whole year and redo them before deciding if surgical intervention was necessary. It was important to see if the leg was gradually correcting itself with normal growth, or not.

On the day of the tests, we took our little son into an examination room where they laid him on a table, asked his father to hold down both of his feet, and asked me to lean across his chest holding his arms and hands still. My head was right next to his face as they took a needle and, without anesthesia, inserted it into the flesh as far as the bone of his calf, and then sent an electric shock through the needle to see if the muscle would respond. Then they took the needle out and reinserted it about ten times in different areas of his leg, trying to determine if the muscle tissue was alive.

You can imagine our son's screams in my ear while his father and I were responsible for holding him down and allowing them to do this to him. I tell you, this is the closest I have ever come to understanding how God must have felt to hold Jesus, His Son, on the cross and allow Him to be hurt because of deformity—but it was my deformity, my sin, not His own! I became even more acutely aware of God's tremendous love while I waited for one year, knowing exactly what my son would endure when they did the tests the second time, and I would be required to help hold him down again. God knew all along what His Son would endure on the cross; but He held Him there—for you and for me!

When it was time for the tests to be repeated, we had moved to live near the city of Dijon in northeastern France, not far from Switzerland. We found another doctor and, after the new tests were performed, he told us there had been no improvement. In his opinion, corrective surgery was our only option. He described the procedure he proposed: cutting our son's leg just below the knee, sawing the tibia in two (the larger of the two bones in the calf), twisting it on its axis to rotate the foot, and then inserting two steel nails to hold it in place while it healed in a cast which would extend from his hip to his toes. Kacha was only two and a half years old, but the doctor said it would be crucial to keep him immobilized during the healing. This meant he would not even be permitted to use crutches or crawl around on the floor. He would have to be kept in a chair from the time he got up in the morning until he went to bed again each night!

The thought of all this was more than Dominique and I could handle. How in the world could we make the decision whether to allow a doctor to cut into the leg of our child? And how could I possibly manage to keep a little boy in a chair all day long, every day, for about nine weeks? Could we trust the doctors? I had no experience with French doctors, but I was already aware that their approach to medical procedures was quite different and generally more aggressive than in the United States. Dominique also had little or no experience with doctors in his country, and we didn't know what to do. We finally told the doctor we couldn't make the decision. We needed time to pray about it. He accepted our choice.

31

I'm not sure how long after that (maybe a couple of weeks), Dominique received a telephone call at his office in France. The man began talking in French, but soon switched to English and Dominique recognized by the accent that he was speaking with an American. The man said his name was Rod Johnston. He had met some people in the States who knew us. He was passing through our area on his way back to Switzerland and wondered if he could stop to see us at our home that evening. Dominique invited him to dinner and came home to tell me we were having a guest.

We shared a wonderful evening of Christian fellowship with Rod. We learned that he and his wife Fran had moved to France 25 years earlier to begin a branch of the Christian youth organization, "Young Life" (Jeunesse Ardente, in French). They were presently living in Annemasse, the French city that borders Geneva, Switzerland. After dinner, Rod left, saying he'd stop back and see us again sometime.

It had been wonderful to spend time relaxing and conversing in English with an American Christian but, after he left, Dominique and I returned to our struggle over the massive decision that loomed in front of us concerning Kacha's leg. I remember so clearly praying, "Lord, if I could have the chance to see a doctor I knew we could trust, and could know whether he agreed with what these French doctors are saying…!" I knew what I was really saying. I was wishing I could go back to the United States to see a doctor there; but, with our financial situation at the time, that was simply not possible.

It wasn't long before we received another telephone call from Rod. This time, Dominique invited him to spend the night. He agreed. After dinner, Rod said to us, "Is there anything you would like me to be praying about for you two?" So we told him about the decision we had to make whether Kacha would have surgery or not. We prayed together and Rod left the next day.

The third time Rod telephoned, he said he and his wife Fran would both be coming through our area on their way back to Annemasse. Then he asked Dominique, "Would you permit us to take Linda and Kacha with us when we leave your home and take them back to Switzerland? We have a friend who is coming to visit from the States and he's a doctor. We talked to him about Kacha's case and, if you bring along all his x-rays and records, the doctor has agreed to look at them, examine Kacha's leg and tell you whether he agrees that you should have the surgery done." Dominique and I agreed that we should go with them.

I will never forget that long drive from Dijon to Geneva through the Alps in the middle of the winter. In the back seat of their car, Kacha's curly, blond head lay in my lap while he slept. We wound through powerful mountain peaks on a road lined with towering pines that glistened with snow sparkling in the moonlight. I remember looking down at our son's peaceful, sleeping face and praying, "Lord, please help us and guide us to know without a doubt whether we should agree to do this surgery."

After spending the rest of the night in Rod and Fran's apartment in Annemasse, the next morning I was surprised to hear we would be driven to the Geneva airport where they had reserved a private room for the doctor to examine Kacha. He was apparently very busy and would only have time perform the examination if he did it at the airport before he left for his next appointment.

Inside the airport, we waited at the gate where the doctor was scheduled to arrive. After his plane landed, I saw Rod and Fran go forward to greet a tall man who came through the door. I stood with Kacha by my side, unable to move because I was so stunned when I recognized the man they were greeting. It was Dr. C. Everett Koop, once the Surgeon General of the United States of America! That was not his position at the time, though. At that time, he was the Chief Surgeon of the Children's Hospital in Philadelphia, Pennsylvania. As he shook my hand when we were introduced, I could hardly speak.

I grew up near Philadelphia. Dr. Koop's reputation as a fine physician, and most of all, as a Christian man who frequently prayed with his patients and their families during medical treatment, was well known. If I had been near Philadelphia with Kacha when we needed to make this decision, this would have been the one man I would have wanted to see above all others. But the chances of getting to see him were often just about impossible. He was so busy and so many people wanted his help. Now, here I was facing the fact that God had known the true desires of my heart—that God had so clearly heard the prayers I had not even dared to put into words—that He had flown this doctor all the way across an ocean, and had arranged for Dr. Koop to meet with our son and help a nobody like me!

Dr. Koop examined our son and agreed that, though they didn't usually intervene surgically to correct this type of deformity, Kacha's case was severe and would not correct itself. He confirmed that we should have the surgery, and I returned to Dijon to tell Dominique how God had answered our prayers. With complete assurance and confidence in God's unmistakable guidance, we went through with our son's surgery.

I've already told you that I believe God is aware of what is happening to you. Had God demonstrated to Dominique and I that He is intimately aware of every detail of our lives? Yes...but further conversations with Rod and Fran Johnston revealed God's provision and care to an extent that we could not have imagined. When we questioned them to know when and where they had been given our address and telephone number, they told us they had been in a church in Kansas raising money for the support of their ministry in France.

We've never been in Kansas, but a couple in that church (who had been hosts to a Young Life group I was associated with during my university studies in Pennsylvania) had moved to Kansas from the Philadelphia area. They apparently approached Rod and Fran, never having met them before or even knowing what part of France they were living in and its proximity to where we lived, and gave them our information, asking if Rod could check in on us and see if we were all right. Then we heard when this meeting had taken place. My friend, God had orchestrated that encounter in Kansas, months before we were even faced with a French doctor asking us for a decision about surgery for our son's leg! God knew our need before we did, and He began to set a series of events into motion that would ultimately provide Dr. C. Everett Koop to confirm a prognosis in Geneva, Switzerland!

Don't you agree that God tenderly, affectionately, and personally cared for us? I can quite honestly say, if someone had come to me during those first tests on our son while I was leaning across his chest and hearing him scream in my ear, and said to me, "Don't worry, Linda, God has this all in hand," I would have been angry with the person for joking or mocking me in the midst of my pain! I would never have believed it would be possible, or that it would happen at all! Why? I've listened to the world. I've listened to Satan.

All of our lives, the world and Satan have been feeding into our minds the very thoughts that stand in the way of simple, childlike trust in God as our Heavenly Father

tenderly caring for us in every circumstance and yearning with deep, sweet love to carry us and keep us through it all!

Messages denying God's love and ridiculing trust in Him as "infantile" and "naïve" have been persistently repeated from every side, piling up one on top of the other, slowly building an enormous barrier that pops up in our minds to block out any glimpse of God's Hand reaching out to us or any understanding of God's ways to provide for us and care for us. The walls of the barrier are built and strengthened by our education system, our news and entertainment media, many of our world leaders, and our judicial, medical and scientific systems—all subtly ingraining their philosophies into our minds until we're convinced it is the natural, normal way to view life.

Their messages are scribbled all over the walls:

"It doesn't make sense to believe God can do anything about this!"

"Why would the God of the universe—if He does exist at all—be concerned about or bother with somebody like you?"

"What have you ever done to expect such special treatment?"

"You're not good enough!"

"You can't count on anybody else, not even God!"

"You can do it on your own! You've got to!"

"What if you pray to Him and then things don't work out? Won't you feel like a fool?"

"You know others who have tried this God-thing, and look what happened to them!"

That's right. It doesn't always make sense, does it? You've seen others pray for God's help, and it didn't seem like anything happened. Things don't always work out, do they? In fact, you may want to say to me, "Fine, Linda. So God sent Dr. Koop. Well, He didn't send a Dr. Koop to me or to my friend. We prayed and my friend still died!—or, my husband still lost his job!—or, my daughter was still raped!—or, my son is still in jail! What difference does it make to pray? What difference does it make to be a Christian? There's still pain! There's still hurt! People still suffer and die!"

Yes, God sent Dr. Koop to us. Yes, God showed us tender care that allowed us to be completely certain we were to have the surgery performed on our son's leg. But I did not tell you he was miraculously restored as a result of that surgery, did I? I did not, because he was not.

Kacha's leg is certainly better than it would have been without the surgery; and today, he is very happy with the level of healing and muscle growth that permits him to enjoy a normal physical life and to excel in the sports he has chosen. As an adult now, he recognizes how difficult it was for us to make the choice for his surgery and he is grateful that it was done.

But God still allowed him to go through the early boyhood years of his life trying to run as fast as other boys and be as capable as his friends in the sports they had chosen. God still asked us to sit on the sidelines of every soccer game and watch our son running half a field away from the rest of his team, trying to keep up with them, trying to be a soccer player like his Papa had been. God still asked us to stand by and watch Kacha try competitive gymnastics, swimming, track and pole-vaulting. God chose not to fulfill Dominique's desire when he prayed over and over as he was out in the sunshine jogging on two powerful, healthy legs that have been granted to him, "Father! If it is Your will, take my legs and give them to my son so that he can be strong the way he wants to be!" Things don't always work out the way we think they should, do they?

We can continue our thinking and push our questions even further. (In fact, you may have already done this sort of thing more than once in your own life). If God could send Dr. Koop all the way over an ocean to reassure us, why couldn't He also have provided another doctor with the wisdom to fix Kacha's leg? I have told you God is powerful and mighty. In fact, I told you I believe God's power stretches beyond the so-called "laws" of medical, physical and mathematical science. So, if He's that powerful and He cares for us so tenderly, why didn't God just heal Kacha's leg completely? Why did God put Kacha and the rest of our family through all that—with, by the way, more surgery later on in Kacha's life?

Kacha gave his heart to God and accepted Jesus Christ as his Savior and Lord when he was six years old. He was raised in a Christian household. Though done imperfectly, Dominique and I love the Lord and sought to nourish our family with the love of God and make known His wonderful deeds every day of Kacha and Fietka's lives.

If God is so powerful and tenderly cares for us, why did He allow Kacha, during his late high school and early college years, to be gradually attracted to a social atmosphere among other young people whose lifestyle and choices of entertainment and pleasure were opposed to, or apathetic towards Christian beliefs and values? Why did God awaken me in the middle of the night, prompting me to go down the hall in our home and stand and pray by Kacha's bed as he thrashed and fought in the torment of horrible dreams, giving me every impression that he was indeed under demonic attack? Why didn't God "wake Kacha up" at that point and cause him to see the danger he was in?

Why did Kacha continue in this lifestyle for two more years? We returned to our home one evening and found him laying on the couch in our living room, terrified and exhausted, not having slept for three days in a row! Trembling and with tears in his eyes, our son tried to explain to us that he wanted to sleep so badly, but every time he laid down to rest and closed his eyes the "voices" tormented him and screamed in his head! He was fearful of being left alone and begged one of us to sleep in the room near him and pray for him. Why did God allow a young man to travel so far into evil territory, that he should come to this point?

Why? Some of the answers have to do with our own choices that we make, don't they? God loves us, but we are not puppets on the end of His strings. He leaves us free to choose to love Him and to follow His way; for without such freedom, our love would be meaningless. If we are not willing to choose His way and listen to His voice, God also leaves us free to hear the other "voices" that will be screaming in our minds.

What you've read so far can also lead you to a commonly asked, but difficult-to-answer question: "Why do bad things happen to good people?" In keeping with the theme of this book, we can build upon that question and ask this one: "If God loves us, why does He let bad things happen to good people?" Or, have you ever had this thought? "If God loves us, then why does He let good things happen to bad people? Why don't the good things happen to us?" Or, as a reaction to the story of our son which I've just shared with you: "If God did all those powerful things when Kacha was a little boy, why didn't He keep on doing powerful things that would have kept you and your son away from trouble and anxiety and heartache?"

If you're willing to be patient and read on to further chapters, we'll spend some time discussing these things and I'll offer several possible answers to our questions that begin with "why." For now, I only want to give you a picture to consider. Which picture? The whole picture.

When you and I don't understand why certain things are happening in our lives, or in the life of someone we love—when we don't see how in the world God could possibly be tenderly caring for us or for them—when it doesn't seem like God hears our prayers or answers them, could it be that things appear this way because we don't see the whole picture, my friend? We do not see as God sees. We do not see what God sees. The Bible tells us, God's ways are far above our ways and His thoughts are far above our thoughts (Isaiah 55:9).

Consider an illustration with me and you might catch a glimpse of what this means. Imagine that I'm standing on a stage or speaker's platform and you're sitting in one of the rows near the front of the auditorium. Now I'm going to unroll a piece of needlework in front of you and hold it up over your head so that you see the back of it, while I stand above you and look down at the front side. As you look at it, I tell you I can see a message in the needlework.

Continuing to hold it above you, I ask you to read the message and tell the rest of the audience what it says. What do you answer? If you have any experience with needlework, you know it's extremely difficult, if not impossible, to see the design clearly when you look at the backside of a piece. So I turn it over and allow you to see it from the front side, from my perspective. Now the message is clear, and you read aloud: "Faith is seeing light with your heart when your eyes see only darkness."

You and I look at our lives, or the lives of those around us, and we see from underneath—from our earthbound perspective—and wonder why such a mess? What is the good of it all? Why this dark line here or that weird color over there? Why does the pattern seem to go off on a tangent in that direction when it would have made more sense to us for it to continue going the other way? We like this part with its quiet, tranquil tones, and can't understand why it seems to be suddenly invaded by a mass of confused, snarled, tangled threads that don't look like they're going anywhere! Though we're thrilled and excited when bright, happy, sun-filled colors explode unexpectedly in one corner, we're soon disappointed to find that they don't last. They soon fade into the somber doldrums of everyday grays. Even when we pause long enough to stop, step back, and consider what's been done so far and where it seems to be going, imagine as we will...we cannot conceive what the picture will be when it's finished!

My friend, God sees our lives from above and knows the reason for the patterns and colors. A message is being woven, and it is the message of your life. In fact, I will go so far as to say that in every person's life there is a message that is being woven. But not all of those messages are the ones God has planned—sometimes not at all, and other times only in part. How can we tell the difference?

I'll answer that question with a question: Who is doing the weaving? Who is holding the threads? Who is choosing the colors and directing the design?

It's hard to let go of the threads of our lives, isn't it? The moment we attempt to trust as a child and let go—putting the threads back into God's Hands—anxiety, worry and fears for the future may flood our thoughts once again. We struggle with the overwhelming urge to grab back what we have surrendered, especially when things start going a bit differently than we might have expected after that bright, brief moment of trust in God.

We wish we could know how it will all turn out. We wish we could be sure. My friend, herein lies the dilemma, yet the very essence of our faith and trust: We will not see the whole picture until we are able to see from above, as God does, from His perspective in Heaven! Until then, we learn to trust God bit by bit and thread by thread, each time a new part of the design comes into view. (Sigh...such a struggle sometimes, right?) But did you happen to notice Father-God's pleasure when you handed over that one thread back there?

"Thinking it through"
(Optional Personal Application)

Let's think about human effort versus God's work. How much of my life have I spent working hard to improve things or change my life because, "If I don't do it, it won't get done! I can't count on [_____], so I might as well get on with life and do things myself!…What? You think somebody else is going to care enough? No way! I've waited on that one before, and it's been a dead-end road! If I don't keep pushing, it will never happen!"

Suggestion: Look up the following verses in the Bible and answer the questions.

Isaiah 41: 9-13…It's just you out there? All alone? What are you afraid of? Who's going to help you? How? _____

_____

_____

_____

_____

_____

Isaiah 49: 14-16…Others have forgotten you, or forgotten their promises to you? Who hasn't forgotten you? How do you know?

_____

_____

_____

_____

_____

Psalm 139: 1-5…So! Nobody else cares what's happening to you? Who else is aware of your life right now? How much? _____

_____

_____

_____

_____

_____

Isaiah 30: 18-21...Are you living through some hard times? Have you been asking around and nobody has answers? Which way to go? Who knows? What exactly is promised to you in these verses? _____

_____

_____

_____

_____

_____

Suggestion: Read aloud the key principle from this chapter, personalizing it.

All of my life, the world and Satan have been feeding into my mind the very thoughts that stand in the way of my own simple, childlike trust in God as my Heavenly Father who tenderly cares for me in every circumstance and yearns with deep, sweet love to carry me and keep me through it all!

Think about the sort of "mental gymnastics" you sometimes go through as you sort your way through issues and decisions in your life. What are some of the thoughts that pop into your mind, which you realize prevent you from simple trust in God? _____

_____

_____

_____

_____

_____

_____

_____

Chapter 5

When Your Life Seems Wasted

In our time together so far, what has God shown us about His plan to help and to heal? First, God wants time with you to repair the damage the world and Satan have done in distorting the image you have of yourself. God must be given permission to reveal the distortions and repair the image, so that you can realize who He created you to be and how He sees you. Then, with a renewed understanding of God's image of you, He can begin to rebuild the internal structures of your heart.

We saw how the world and Satan have worked throughout the past to cause us to focus on the frame and become so distraught, trying to measure up to the world's demands and seek its approval, that we neglect and ignore the true value of life: the unique message of each heart and mind and soul. We've been focusing on the wrong thing, haven't we? God must pivot our perspective so we spend less time fretting and fussing over the frame and spend more time with Him—alone with Him—learning to know Him and love Him, learning to turn our eyes away from the frame and look to Him, learning to trust that the work He is doing in our hearts is good and that it will finish well.

God has described Himself (and wants you to see Him and accept Him) as the Great Creator, the Designer who uniquely and purposefully fashioned you. Accepting Him as your Creator and Designer means you will begin to see things in your life differently. God becomes the Revealer, His light revealing His character in love more clearly than you have ever seen before.

But that same light also shines over your life and your heart and reveals God's perspective of what is there. To help you deal with what you see and to give you strength to surrender the wreckage, God becomes the Comforter. Trembling in fear and dragging yourself forward (or stiffening your back and gritting your teeth), pushing on towards God and expecting to meet the Judge, you may be surprised to see God the Mediator and Savior instead.

Yes, there must be judgment. Yes, sin must be dealt with. Jesus holds up the ancient, old-looking key—the key from times beyond your time, the key that has existed from the beginning of time—and declares

His power to unlock the chains that keep you bound to your past, bound to be who you have always been, preventing you from becoming who God sees you to be. Yes, sin must be dealt with before you meet Father-God. Jesus the Son of God, Jesus the Mediator and Savior explains that it has already been dealt with!

But if we are willing come to meet Father-God in a prayer encounter such as this, what will happen to our past? What will God do with it? Well, we don't have to wonder. God gives us a beautiful picture of what He will do once we trust in Him. The picture of God's plan and promise is found in the Old Testament, in chapter 2 of the book of the prophet Joel. (If you have a Bible, you might want to get it and follow along.)

Verse 23 begins, *"So rejoice, O sons of Zion..."* Who are the sons of Zion? When this was originally written, it referred to the people of Israel, the Jews, who were known as God's people. But today this also means anybody who is a Christian, because every person who becomes a Christian is then one of God's sons or daughters and has become a member of the family of God. Now all who trust in Jesus Christ as Savior and Lord are God's people.

"And be glad in the LORD your God..." the verse continues. What are we to be glad about, once we have put our trust in Father-God and have accepted the work of Jesus Christ? *"...For He has given you the early rain for your vindication..."* The early rain mentioned here is also translated "the teacher for righteousness." Once we come back to God and trust in His work in our lives, He will give us "the early rain" (the teacher of righteousness).

Who is this teacher? Who is the One who is promised in the New Testament to teach us righteousness? *"But the Helper, the Holy Spirit, whom the Father will send in My name, He will teach you all things, and bring to your remembrance all that I said to you"* (John 14:26). Who is this teacher of righteousness? The Holy Spirit. Now that you are among God's people, a son or daughter of God, you can expect that the Holy Spirit will begin to teach you about living rightly with God and how to walk in His ways of righteousness.

Righteousness—that's a big "church-word," isn't it? You may have a vague, sort of fuzzy-good feeling about what righteousness means and know that it's something like "being good," but it might become clearer if you look at another Bible-person, a man called Job, and how he is described. This description of Job is important because God considered

43

Job to be righteous. *"There was a man…whose name was Job, and that man was* **blameless, upright, fearing God, and turning away from evil"** (Job 1:1).

"Blameless! Upright! Fearing God! Turning away from evil! God wants to teach me how to be all that? Wow! Sure sounds like He's got a lot of work to do, because I'm nowhere near all that! In fact, I take a look at who I am today and where I am in life now, and it sure looks like it's going to take some hard, hard work to get me from point A to point B! Ouch! This could even hurt!" Ah, my friend! If that is your reaction, you do not yet know enough about the character of Father-God and our teacher of righteousness, the Holy Spirit! Look back to the prophet Joel's description of this teacher (the "rain").

"And He has poured down for you the rain, the early and latter rain as before" (verse 23). The "early rain" refers to a spring rain and the "latter rain" refers to an autumn rain. Tell me, what are spring and autumn rains often like? They are soft, gentle, sprinkling rains that quietly water the earth, washing it and soaking it with health-giving moisture. Now do you have a different picture in your mind of how this teaching from the Holy Spirit is intended to benefit us and help us to grow?

If you allow the Holy Spirit to instruct you after you've decided to trust God with your life, what will happen to you? Look at verse 24. *"And the threshing floors will be full of grain, and the vats will overflow with the new wine and oil."* What is grain used for? In those days, it was a crop that was used to make bread. This tells us that trusting God can lead to lives that are filled up with the fruit of God's promises and nourished by the Spirit of Jesus Christ, who is the Bread of Life. We will see an overflowing of new wine through us, which (throughout the New Testament of the Bible) is the symbolic representation of the grace of God at work in a repentant heart. And the oil mentioned here refers to the Holy Spirit. There will be evidence of God's grace in your life. There will be evidence of the power of the Holy Spirit working in and through your life. Not just some evidence. God promises us it will be overflowing!

So far, all of this is talking about what will happen to us in the present, once we've trusted God and turned our hearts toward Him. But, now we return to our original question: What about my past? Look at what God plans to do about that! *"Then I will make up to you for the years that the swarming locust has eaten, the creeping locust, the stripping locust, and the gnawing locust…"* (verse 25).

What is God going to do about the hurt you've known in the past? He's going to bless you so much that it will make up for it! God says, "I will make up to you for the years…eaten!" You will be comforted according to the time that you have been afflicted. Your years of famine shall be replaced by years of plenty. Do you see how God is aware of every detail, how He knows exactly what happened to you, how Father-God cares so sympathetically for you?

As has so often happened before, once again I see that not a word of the Bible was written randomly or by accident. They are each chosen with purpose and design, and sometimes reveal that God's sense of humor surprises me when I least expect it. When I was studying and preparing to write this material, I came across these descriptions of the locusts that had been eating up my past, and I sat back and laughed. Let me tell you why.

Look at the first one: "the swarming locusts." Do you remember what the swarming locusts were in our lives? The Junior High herd mentality! Haven't you ever noticed that junior-highers (adolescents from about 11-14 years old) seem to travel in herds? They're always in a group! They never walk anywhere alone. And can they ever swarm! Watch them at a group event sometime (like a football game, for instance). They are capable of swarming their little group around the victim for the day and stinging that poor person to death with their words and their looks! Remember?

And "the creeping locusts." Do you know what they were? Those were the creeps that tried to slither into our lives and have their own way with our minds or bodies, and use up our emotions. When they had finished filling themselves up at our expense and puffing themselves up with the pride of another conquest, they strutted back out of our lives. For some of us, this continued all the way through our teenage and college or university years, and beyond!

When the creeps left, "the stripping locusts" showed up. Unfortunately, by this time in life, these locusts had learned to be subtle. They recognized the damage done by the creeps and knew we were probably starting to "wise up," so they knew they had to work more slowly—getting us to trust them or even to marry them before we realized that their real agenda was to strip us in physical abuse and use our bodies for their own desires, or strip us in verbal abuse so that we lost all self-respect, or strip our bank accounts so that we lost everything we owned, or strip us of our children by turning them against us and luring them away into things that alienate us further and further from each other.

By now, I had stopped laughing. It's not so funny anymore, is it— especially when you realize what happens next? Which locusts show up in our lives when the swarming locusts and the creeping locusts and the stripping locusts get done with us? "The gnawing locusts." That gnawing feeling of betrayal, guilt, pain, emptiness and meaninglessness—wondering if you can trust anyone anymore, and whether it's even worth it to try! Wondering where you're headed in life and what you have to look forward to—that gnawing feeling of futility. God says, "I know. I saw it all. Come to Me and I will make up to you for the damage that has been done in the times you have suffered!"

How is God going to make it up to you? *"You shall have plenty to eat and be satisfied, and praise the name of the LORD your God, who has dealt wondrously with you; then you will never be put to shame. You will know that I am in your midst, and that I am the LORD your God and there is no other; and you will never again be put to shame!"* (verse 26, 27). You will never again be put to shame! That's how God is going to make it up to you! That's how God is going to protect you! That's how God is going to change your life!

The totally unproductive, vast, dry, empty wasteland of your past…what's God going to do with it? He's going to redeem it and make it up to you, remaking it and changing it into something useful by transforming YOU! As you allow God to pivot your perspective in life and turn your eyes upon Him, looking to Him for guidance and strength to follow His righteous ways, looking to His Word for wisdom and discernment in the choices and decisions you must make each day, God will continue His work to repair and rebuild your heart!

He describes His desires for us, describing exactly the work He intends to do in our hearts. *"[The LORD] will comfort all [your] waste places. And [your] wilderness He will make like Eden, and [your] desert like the garden of the LORD; joy and gladness will be found in [you], thanksgiving and the sound of a melody"* (Isaiah 51:3, emphasis mine). God will cause the wilderness and the desert that was your life to bloom! *"The wilderness and the desert will be glad, and the [desert] will rejoice and blossom; like the crocus it will blossom profusely and rejoice with rejoicing and shout of joy…and the scorched land will become a pool, and the thirsty ground springs of water…"* (Isaiah 35:1,2,7).

God intends to make your life bloom and be fruitful! He can take that which was ugly, dirty, scroungy and scrappy, and turn it into a garden of beautiful blossoms and gorgeous, vibrant, colorful fruits and flowers! God can take what was lifeless and dead, even that which was poisoning you in its rottenness and decay, and cleanse it and make it come back to life, with new life!

Please don't read these words I've written and think I don't know what I'm talking about because you think I'm a Christian teacher who has had a protected life and can't have a clue what your life is like (or what real life is like, for that matter)! I don't even remember the names and faces of all the men I had sex with before I was a Christian and before I married my husband! I might not know what your life looks like behind closed doors, but I know what mine was like before I trusted God, and what it is like now. I know what is true.

God did repair my heart. God did rebuild my heart. God did refill my heart…and He continues to do so—making a garden from a wasteland, and recreating a life of joy and love and incredible peace from what was a hellish existence of stupidity, lust and greed! I am certain God did this in my life, and I am certain He can do it in your life, too. I'll say it again:

God can take that which was lifeless and dead, and make it come back to life, with NEW life!

Ask another Bible-person named Ezekiel what he saw happen to a valley full of dry bones! The story is found in the Old Testament in the book of the prophet Ezekiel, chapter 37 and verses 1-14. Before we look at the account itself, it's helpful to realize the historical context of this story which was written to describe and respond to the hopeless state of the nation of Israel at that time. Their situation closely resembles yours, if your life seems so hopeless, ruined, and empty that you are convinced God cares nothing for you and has turned His back on you.

The Israelites were dispersed among their enemies and in captivity. They considered themselves destitute of help to enable their return to their own lands. They were generally dispirited in their minds and basically comparing themselves to a bunch of dry bones. *"Our bones are dried up, and our hope has perished. We are completely cut off,"* they said (verse 11).

What about you? Do you feel trapped in a situation in your life and can't imagine how you could ever be free to start over again and get back to what your life was like when things were good, before you got tangled up in the mess you're facing? When you look at yourself, do you feel like things have gone so far that you see no possible way for it to change? Is it so complicated that you can see no way out? Have you given up and decided to accept that your life is ruined? When you read my words declaring that God can make a beautiful garden of your life, did you look around you and think, "How could anyone make something good out of this?"

I invite you to bring all those thoughts and questions along with you, and come with me to read what happened to Ezekiel. His story begins this way: *"The hand of the LORD was upon me, and He brought me out by the Spirit of the LORD and set me down in the middle of the valley; and it was full of bones. And he caused me to pass among them round about, and behold, there were very many on the surface of the valley; and lo, they were very dry"* (Ezekiel 37: 1,2).

Have you ever seen a skeleton? Was it made of real bones or imitation ones? How did it make you feel? How do you suppose Ezekiel felt as he looked out over this valley? He saw a valley of dead men's bones, human bones—not all piled together, but scattered all around on the ground as if a battle had been fought there and the bodies had been left unburied, had putrefied, and now only the bones were left. And these bones were disjointed and strewn all about. Imagine the sense of desolation and destruction which must have overwhelmed Ezekiel's mind and spirit as he looked out across the wide floor of that valley and saw, this was all that remained of human lives! Do you sense the same desolation and destruction when you look back through the valley of your own life?

Ezekiel observed there were not only many bones, they were also very…what? Dry! Why might their dryness be significant? Healthy bones are normally moistened by marrow, aren't they? But these bones had been disjointed and exposed to the sun and wind for so long that they had become dry as dust.

"And [God] said to [Ezekiel], 'Son of man, can these bones live?' And I answered, 'O LORD GOD, Thou knowest' (verse 3). Can life exist here again? Can these bones with their marrow, the very essence of their life, sucked up and dried out of them—can these bones that once formed human bodies, but are now ripped apart and scattered all over the place in a complicated mess, possibly be brought back together to form a life worth living again? Can yours?

First, God wanted Ezekiel to recognize the condition as desperate, and then to admit that man's designs of philosophy, science, industry, governments and politics (and yes, even religion in a dead, strictly intellectual form) are powerless to remedy the situation. All must be referred to God as the only counsel or power sufficient.

"Can these bones live? Can life be restored?"

The blunt, childlike frankness of Ezekiel's response defines man's limitations and admits what is beyond him. "God, You know. I don't know. I don't know if these bones can be made to live again, or how; but I know that You know." With these words, Ezekiel has stooped and humbly drawn a line in the sandy floor of the valley once filled with life—admitting man's limited boundary of knowledge and power, and recognizing the infinite stretch beyond as that which belongs to God alone.

Again [God] said to me, "Prophesy [declare the truth of God's Word] *over these bones, and say to them, 'O dry bones, hear the word of the LORD. Thus says the LORD GOD to these bones, "Behold I will cause breath to enter you that you may come to life. And I will put sinews on you, make flesh grow back on you, cover you with skin, and put breath in you that you may come alive; and you will know that I am the LORD."*

So I prophesied as I was commanded; and as I prophesied, there was a noise, and behold, a rattling; and the bones came together, bone to its bone [bones coming back together again in order, each finding its proper place in the body, restored to its place as it was originally created and designed]. *And I looked, and behold, sinews were on them, and flesh grew, and skin covered them* [God restored and rebuilt the physical structure, reestablishing it in all its practical detail]; *but there was no breath in them.*

Then [God] said to me, "Prophesy to the breath, prophesy, son of man, and say to the breath, 'Thus says the LORD GOD, Come from the four winds, O breath, and breathe on these slain, that they come to life [in Hebrew, the words breath, wind, and spirit are all the same word].' *So I prophesied as He commanded me, and the breath came into them* [God restored the spiritual life], *and they came to life, and stood on their feet* [restored, not wobbly and faint and sickly, but returned to STRENGTH!], *an exceedingly great army.*

Then [God] said to me, "Son of man, these bones are the whole house of Israel; behold they say, 'Our bones are dried up, and our hope has perished. We are completely cut off.' [Interesting! They probably thought, as you may have, that God had turned His back on them and wasn't even aware of what they were going through. God had listened to what they said. God had heard their thoughts. God listens. God hears.]

Therefore, prophesy, and say to them, 'Thus says the LORD GOD, "Behold, I will open your graves and cause you to come up out of your graves, My people [God can deliver you out of the entrapment of deadly sin strangling you and smothering the life out of you]; *and I will bring you into the land of Israel* [God can restore you and return you to take your stand and fill the role of His design in your life].

Then you will know that I am the LORD, when I have opened your graves and caused you to come up out of your graves, My people. And I will put My Spirit within you [the teacher of righteousness, the promise of the Holy Spirit, the early and the latter rains, remember?], *and you will come to life, and I will place you on your own land. Then you will know that I, the LORD, have spoken and done it," declares the LORD* (verses 4-14).

Who but God can do such things? With the knowledge and instruments that medical science has acquired, physicians can reconnect a limb, but who can breathe life back into the spirit? Who can give the will and desire to live? God the Creator and Designer who so fearfully and wonderfully made us, can, in like manner, re-make us! With electrical stimulus and shock treatment, the human heart can be forced to pump again when it stops because of physical trauma. But who can restore the heart to love again?

History records the return of the Jews (here envisioned), though scattered in several parts of Babylon. They returned to find their respective families and re-establish those bonds once severed. When troubles continue long, when hopes have been often frustrated, and when all of your own confidences have failed, is it not time to pray and admit what you cannot do, and turn to the One True God? Or you may have already repented of your past but, regretting the foolishness of your mistakes and living with the guilt of your errors, you're still wishing it had never happened and find it hard to believe anything good will ever come of it.

My friend, see these bones that God brought back together again when Ezekiel prayed! See your life, your past—a different time, a different place, the same God—waiting to restore, waiting for one thing...your prayer.

"Thinking it through"
(Optional Personal Application)

Suggestion: Go back to God's promise that He will "make up to you for the years that the swarming locust has eaten, the creeping locust, the stripping locust, and the gnawing locust…" Consider your past.

What were the swarming locusts? _____
_____

How would you describe the creeping locusts? _____
_____

What happened when the stripping locusts came? _____
_____

What does the gnawing locust do in your life? _____
_____

Suggestion: Ask God to forgive you for the time when you allowed the locusts to have their own way in your life; and ask Him to heal you from the times when their destruction was forced upon you. Say the following aloud, personalizing it and allowing yourself to take hope from the promise that is offered:

"God will make up to me for the years that were eaten. I shall be comforted according to the time that I have been afflicted."

Suggestion: In Ezekiel's vision of the valley of dry bones, God promises to restore them. He gets specific in that promise. Look at each part God promises to do, and decide how God would do that in your own life if He were given permission by you to restore it (or as He has already done).

"I will cause breath to enter you…" _____

_____

_____

_____

"I will put sinews on you…" _____

_____

_____

_____

"I will make flesh to grow back on you…" _____

_____

_____

_____

"I will cover you with skin…" _____

_____

_____

_____

"I will put breath in you that you may come alive…" _____

_____

_____

_____

Suggestion: The KEY principle that was highlighted in this chapter makes an astounding claim. Read it again, aloud this time.

God can take that which was lifeless and dead, and make it come back to life, with NEW life!

Focus particularly on the last phrase. God is not promising to simply FIX your life. He's promising to make something NEW! Do you believe He can…He will?

Chapter 6

When Life Is Too Full

God is at work repairing our hearts. The deepest inner part of us is being restructured and rebuilt in order to recreate a sanctuary for God in our hearts. A sanctuary! That's surely a word you've heard before. How would you describe in your own words, a sanctuary? What type of place is it? Listen to this definition I found: A sanctuary is the most sacred part of a place that is a sacred structure. It was also described as a place of refuge or asylum, a place we can retreat to and feel protected and safe.

Think about the first definition: A sanctuary is the most sacred part of a place that is a sacred structure. God wants to create a sanctuary of our hearts. Isn't my heart the most sacred part of me? Isn't your heart the most sacred part of you? And now that I'm a child of God, a Christian, God's own daughter, am I not a sacred structure? The Bible tells me that I am *"...being built up as a spiritual house for a holy priesthood, to offer up spiritual sacrifices acceptable to God through Jesus Christ...a royal priesthood...a people for God's own possession..."* (I Peter 2:5,9). All this is gradually becoming a reality in my life as God repairs my heart. That sounds like a sacred structure, to me.

God wants your heart to become the most sacred part of you! What does "sacred" mean? It refers to that which is set apart or dedicated to be used only in the matters of your faith. It is inviolable, meaning it is not to be violated in any way with anything that is contrary to your faith. Put all these ideas together when we say God wants to create a sanctuary of your heart, and we can now see that God wants to create in you a heart that is set apart and dedicated to be used only in matters that do not violate or damage or interrupt your walk with Him.

You may be thinking, "That sounds so holy! How am I ever going to be like that?"

Learn to love God. Learn to love Him more than you do today. Learn to know God. Learn to know Him more than you do today. How do you do that? The same way you do with anyone else: spend time with Him. Spend more time with Him than you have been doing.

54

I'll make this more personal, and maybe it will help you understand how vital this is.

I know my husband and love him more than anyone else does, even those of our family and close personal friends who also know him and love him. But I'm certain I know my husband and love him more than any of those persons. Why? How can I be so sure? I've spent more time with him than anyone else has! It's just that simple.

I once heard a Christian teacher say he is convinced that if more Christians worked diligently to study the Scriptures and read books about the Bible which expressly seek to reveal the character of God, we would have less weakness and failure in our lives, and there would be greater strength in the witness of God's Church to the world around us. In like manner, I have studied my husband's personality and character, and I have learned to love him and trust him, culminating in the constant, daily desire to serve him and please him.

In fact, I've become so inspired by the man my husband seeks to be that I want other men to know him and learn from him, so I'm constantly lifting up his name and holding him up as someone to turn to for counsel and to follow his example. And yet he does these things imperfectly, doesn't he? He is frail. He is human. He fails.

I have also studied God's personality and character. He is not frail. He is not human. He does not fail. How much more will I gain in strength and confidence as I spend time with my Heavenly Father and learn the infinite extent to which I can absolutely rely upon, resolutely count on, and constantly depend upon His unchanging love and affectionate care towards me?

Do you know what times I love most with my husband? Our "alone-times," when it's just the two of us. God loves you. He's your Father. Even if you haven't yet allowed Him that role in your life, He still wants to be your Father. He wants alone-times with you, too. Why? Why are alone-times so important to us?

As I write this book, we're now living in Spain. As soon as we moved here, we contacted a young, Spanish woman who lived with us several years ago in Michigan as a foreign exchange student during her senior year in high school. We've only seen Raquel once since she left our Michigan home to return to Spain. But we will never forget, and neither does she, the moment when she asked to kneel beside our bed with us and ask Jesus Christ to forgive her sins. She had come to understand her great desire to love God and be loved by Him. We had spent many, many hours of alone-time with Raquel, listening to her heart and opening our hearts to her, as well.

When she telephoned us, ecstatic that we are now living in Spain and excitedly making arrangements to come to see us in our new home here, I suggested that she could come with some of her friends if she wished. "No, Leeeenda! I want to be alone with just you and Domingo!" (That's her Spanish way of saying our names.) After all this time, what does she want most? To be ALONE with us. Why? She wants to feel completely free to share her heart with us and hear from our hearts, as well.

Alone-times. How important they are with those we love! Why should our desire for alone-time with God be any different, any less? Why not more so? We have lots of together-times with others in our lives, don't we? In fact, we have so many together-times, that this is exactly the reason why God knows we need the alone-times with Him.

The things God has in store to share with us in alone-times with Him are meant to prepare us for the together-times with others which He knows are coming.

Come away with God to these alone-times and, when He's satisfied with the work you've allowed Him to do repairing and rebuilding more of your heart in that one bit of time together with Him, then He'll tell you to open the door and go out to do your together-times with others. But you'll go out with treasure stored in your heart, enabling you to face the together-times with others—both those that are easy and fun and full of peace, and those that are...well, not so easy or fun.

Why is this so important, so vital in the rebuilding of your heart? In order to allow God to rebuild your heart, you must learn to trust Him. In order to learn that you can trust God, you must spend time with Him in His Presence. Yearn to spend time with Father-God, and you will discover that your "trusting-place" is in those quiet times where you meet with Him alone. You will begin to treasure those times each day and that spot in your life where you meet with Him alone.

The world can be waiting right outside; you will gradually realize it's better to let it wait. You are better prepared to serve it when you have first been with the One who taught us service by laying down His life.

The world can be knocking at your door. You will better respond when you have first been with the One who shows us how to discern true need and how to see beyond present, pressing issues and see into the heart.

The world can even be sitting there watching. You will have learned the wisdom of retreating from it and ignoring its demands, even its pleasures, until you have answered the call to be with your Father.

Your Father wants to be alone with you. Do you yearn to be alone with Him? Do you look forward to that time each day? Go to be alone with God—alert, eager, contented, relaxed, but excited with anticipation and happy to close the door behind you! Create a place where you can do that. I mean that literally.

We have moved our home to live in another place (another state or another country) 16 times since we were married 30 years ago. Each time we move, I face the enormous task of setting up housekeeping again, recreating what I call our "hole-in-the-world"—our place to retreat and relax. I know that once we're settled, the guests will start to arrive. They always do. Why? Because we've invited them!

Those who have taken us at our word and come to spend a week or two with us have, for the most part, been sufficiently served and pleased with the hospitality we offer that they've gone home to spread the word! This is wonderful, because to us this means we're successfully serving God in sharing the blessings of the home He has provided for us, and we know this pleases Him. It is also means the guests keep coming, and I smile to think of the many entries in our guest book already.

This also means that personal privacy can become an issue. It means I must make a special effort, when we have guests staying overnight for a week or two at a time, if I want to get away to a place where I can have alone-time with Father-God each day. So, by now, my husband knows when we find our new home, and start to decide which room will serve which purpose and begin arranging furniture in those rooms accordingly, I will carefully arrange things to create a new alone-spot (usually in our bedroom) where I can close the door and retreat, no matter who else might be around or what else might be going on. He'll come to me with a quiet grin on his face and say, "I see you've found your spot again."

Yes, he saw the same chair, a little table brought next to the chair, the devotional and study books placed beside my Bible, the pen and marker and notepad used to remember what I learn, the same three pictures placed on the little table (one of our daughter Fietka and her boyfriend Rob, one of our son Kacha and his wife Michelle, and one of my husband), the prayer-request list from others tucked under my Bible, the same afghan thrown over the back of the chair for cold, wintry days, the same little stool to prop up my feet.

Yes, I have recreated my spot. He knows it. Our children know it. Before long, guests that come to visit also know this is my spot to be alone with God. Why? Is it forbidden territory for them? No. At some time or another, they've come to speak with me and found me there. We talk. But before long they leave again…not without me noticing a quiet look of pleasure on their faces, realizing full well why I'm there and what I'm doing, and happy in what they've seen.

It is good to purposefully and deliberately make a place like this for yourself in the space where you live. It becomes a physical reminder each day that Father-God is waiting and wanting to meet alone with you. It becomes a physical reminder to others (your children, your extended family, and your guests) that it is a good thing to quietly, diligently, purposefully, and with systematic discipline, study the Bible and pray—alone with God.

While we were living in England, I was sitting alone in the office in our home one day typing an email to our daughter Fietka. I was trying to describe to her how much Father-God wants to be alone with her, and wants her to stop everything else and sit down to concentrate on her time with Him, just Him. I knew it would help her to grasp this more fully if she would think of her Papa. She and Dominique have a very close, healthy, loving relationship. But now that we're living in Europe, the times we have together are more limited. I asked her to think about how much she'd love to have time with her Papa right now. This is what I wrote to her:

"Couldn't you see yourself happy to sit down next to him, cuddle up in the crook of his arm, snuggle your nose into the soft parts of his cheek, and then sigh a huge sigh of relief and feel your whole body relax in the comfort and joy of being there with him? You're relaxed, and yet you sense every part of you is excited to be near him and anxious to hear what he's going to say next, right? Of course, that's right. You've experienced it so many times in your life already, haven't you, Fietka? And I know you're smiling with tears in your eyes right now, just thinking about it as you read this. It's good for you to feel this way about your Papa. But my sweet daughter, this is exactly how your Heavenly Father wants you to feel about time with Him, too. This is how your Heavenly Father feels about time with you!"

God has given me a new understanding of His desire to be alone with me, and His desire to be with each of His children. We are His children! Do we understand that? How much does He love us and want us to be alone with Him? One Sunday when we were worshipping in our church in England, I suddenly realized more poignantly than ever before in my life what God must feel when He misses us and yearns to spend time with us.

During the service, I suddenly noticed someone come in through the door, arriving late to the worship service. When the person recognized a friend already seated and that person noticed her standing there, they both broke out in big smiles and she went to sit with the one she knew. In that short moment, I realized how I'd feel if suddenly my daughter or son or daughter-in-law appeared at the door. I was happy for those I didn't know that day. But what I would have felt if I had looked up and instead saw Fietka, or Kacha, or Michelle!

In fact, some people have had the opportunity to see that joy explode on my face and tears of surprised happiness stream down my face when I looked up and saw our daughter Fietka and our daughter-in-law Michelle come through the door when I least expected it. I was invited to be the speaker at a retreat in Michigan while we were living in England. I was happy to accept the invitation, but soon felt a growing sadness in my heart that though I would be so much closer to our daughter who was living in North Carolina at the time, I would still not see her since she couldn't afford to come to Michigan and attend the retreat with us. I was saddened even further when our daughter-in-law Michelle told me she had other plans and also would not be able to spend the weekend with me.

God heard the quiet, sad longings of my heart. He then laid those same thoughts on my friend Carolynn's heart. Carolynn was in charge of organizing this retreat and, as a surprise, to thank me for coming all the way from England to teach at this event, she secretly contacted Fietka and made arrangements for her to attend, paying for her flight to join us.

Friday night, I was already enjoying the fellowship and fun of being back in America with a crowd of Christian sisters that were laughing and talking with me before the first speaking session began, when suddenly someone touched my shoulder and said, "Linda, look," pointing across the room. And there stood my daughter Fietka, my daughter-in-law Michelle, and Michelle's mother Janet (one of my best friends), side by side! Everyone watched how quickly I flew across the room and wrapped my arms around all three of them, squishing them with my hugs, smooshing kisses on their cheeks, and spilling my tears all over them! Why? Because they are my children! They are my family!

We feel so far away from them, now that we're living in Europe and they live in the United States! Obviously, we don't get to see them very often, maybe two or three times a year at most. How precious times with them have become! I yearn for moments when we can talk together on the telephone, and look forward to times when we can actually be together, and hug each other, and walk arm-in-arm, and talk face-to-face. When they come to see us, I watch them leave afterwards at the airport, already looking forward to the next time we can be together again.

Why? Why do I feel differently about them than I do about someone else coming through the door? Because they are our children! I miss our friends, too. Certainly I'm excited and happy when I can anticipate the time we'll spend with dear friends who come to visit us. But I can easily admit, none of those times thrill me and fill my heart like the thought of a vacation with our own children, our own family.

That Sunday morning in England, in the midst of my emotions about missing our children, a thought struck me like a thunderbolt: "This is exactly how my Heavenly Father feels about me! This is how much He yearns to see my face, to see me walk through the door and spend time with Him alone!"

Is it beginning to happen? Is God beginning to pivot your perspective and turn your eyes from the world and from people around you—constantly wondering what they think of you and whether they "like" you, and constantly reviewing the damage the world and Satan have caused in your life—to look instead toward Him, toward Father-God?

So many have asked me, begged Dominique and me to give them assurance that somebody loves them. How assured do you feel when someone you know and admire says he or she wants to spend time alone with you to get to know you better? "I want to be alone with you, just the two of us!" Do you remember how it felt to hear those words?

Now here I am telling you that God Himself wants to be alone with you—wants you to know His heart of love towards you. It is the time for you to answer your own question.

"Does anybody love me, simply and genuinely love me and want me for who I really am?"

And Father-God is leaning forward from His Throne, stretching His gaze down the gap of eternity separating heaven and earth, eagerly anticipating the answer He has longed for...

"Thinking it through"
(Optional Personal Application)

Suggestion: This is a tool to help you get deeper into some thinking-time with the Bible. Read the example below, and then try this exercise yourself using the verse that's written out afterwards. We can greatly benefit from taking the time to think carefully about each word in a Bible verse. Think about what the words mean, how they apply to your own life, how they become a reality, how you live them out or desire to do so. Write down the thoughts that come to your mind, expanding on the meaning of one word or phrase at a time. Here's the example:

Romans 12:2— *"And do not be conformed to this world, but be transformed by the renewing of your mind…"*

And do not be conformed…a command—something we are NOT to do—something we are not to allow to happen to us—not allow myself to be molded and shaped, changed to fit the same shape—not allow myself to be pushed and forced into a position that is not true of my deepest inner self

to this world…those things that are not of God—that are only of the horizontal dimension we live in here on earth—that is devoid of any of the spiritual realm of heaven—of those things that will be at enmity with God—to those things and people that will not agree with the commands and precepts of Scripture—to those things and people that will be on the easiest road—the most comfortable way of least resistance

but be transformed…passive verb—meaning, something I allow to be done to me, not something I do to myself—not just a change of shape on the outside, but a total remake from the inside out—from the heart, not just of the mind—a change that affects the very fiber of my being—that must of necessity carry out into every single arena of my life—else, there is not a true transformation that has indeed made of me a new creation—a gradual process, but lasting because it is so thorough *by the renewing...*the wiping clean—the making new of something—a rendering that restores to original quality in its fullest and purest sense—a restoring to how it was created and intended to function—a revitalization of power and strength in clarity

*of your mind...*not my body, but the very core of my thoughts— the deepest private part of me that few, or perhaps none ever discover— the parts I used to hide, but now freely give over to God knowing He has known what is there all along and wanting to be done with those things I now realize are not pleasing to Him—realigning my abilities to reason, discern, and yes, even to rationalize under God's tender care— willingly submitting my mental life to the direction, correction, and guidance of God's sweet Spirit.

Suggestion: If this has touched your heart as you read through the example, you might read it aloud again, praying it back to God this time, as the true desire of your own heart. This is what often happens when we use this tool.

Suggestion: Now take some paper and try the same exercise with the verse below that's already broken into significant phrases for you. (You can continue with other verses and make this a regular part of your alone-time, if you wish.)

Jeremiah 29:11— *"For I know the plans that I have for you, declares the LORD, plans for welfare and not for calamity to give you a future and a hope."*

For I know..._____

_____

_____

_____

Linda Azema

the plans…_____

_____

_____

_____

that I have…_____

_____

_____

_____

for you…_____

_____

_____

_____

declares the LORD,…_____

_____

_____

_____

plans for welfare…_____

_____

_____

_____

and not for calamity…_____

_____

_____

_____

to give..._____

_____

_____

_____

you..._____

_____

_____

_____

a future..._____

_____

_____

_____

and a hope._____

_____

_____

_____

Suggestion: If this seems like a lot of work to you, remind yourself of the key principle of this chapter. Read it aloud again now, and ask yourself how an exercise like the one we've just looked at could help you discover greater depth in your alone-times with God, and open new meaning to you as you read the Bible.

The things God has in store to share with me in alone-times with Him are meant to prepare me for the together-times with others which He knows are coming.

Chapter 7

When No One Can Tell You Why

I promised you we would get back to the why-questions. The events of life that force us to ask "why" can leave us shaken. Unanswered why-questions can make us falter in our faith or even bring us to the brink of fading faith, can't they?

As one friend has expressed to me, "I feel like I'm walking along a knife edge, staring down into an abyss on either side, wobbling and teetering on the edge of a precipice. I could so easily let myself slip off the edge away from faith in God."

She knows there is only a gray fog of nothingness there (over the edge, away from faith in God), but at least in nothingness she hopes her mind will stop asking questions. Or she must abandon her why-questions and jump off the other side, trusting that God will somehow answer her desperate leap toward stubborn faith and respond to her with such love that her unanswered questions will...not matter? No. Our why-questions will always matter, answered or unanswered. She will simply be given peace to wait for the answers, to wait until she sees the whole picture.

Why do bad things happen to good people?

Why does God allow bad people to use us and hurt us?

Why doesn't God change those bad people?

Why does God allow sickness and physical pain and disease and death, even what we would call premature death that we aren't prepared to face?

It seems like God heals some people. Why doesn't He heal everyone who prays to Him and asks for His help?

Why doesn't God intervene and protect us, or the ones we love, from dangers and temptations and evil influences? He does, sometimes.

Why not all the time?

Why not every time?

Why does it seem like some people hear personally from God, hear His voice, and yet He remains silent when others beg to hear from Him?

How can we be expected to accept that God loves us, without these why-questions being answered?

You will remember part of the answer to these why-questions that I gave you already. Sometimes bad things happen to good people because of the choices we make. The difficult circumstances you and I might be living through can sometimes be directly traced back to wrong, selfish choices we made somewhere in the past. Then we must live with the consequences of our foolish, rash, or immature behavior.

Sometimes bad things happen to good people because good people make bad choices. So far, this is the easiest answer to accept when we tackle our why-questions. Why? Been there, done that. All of us.

Now it gets tougher. Good people (innocent from any wrong choice of their own) can be hurt or attacked by evil people who are carrying out the action of their own bad choices, and the good people are victims of someone else's evil behavior. You've got a painful, personal memory resurfacing in your mind right now, don't you? Or headlines from today's news flash into focus as you're reading this. Every day, any day. It happens all the time. Why? If God is all-powerful and all-knowing (which He is), why doesn't He stop it? Why doesn't He intervene? Why does He just let those things happen?

I don't know. But I'm convinced of this: I *will* know. Someday, I will see all things clearly. There will come a day in my life when I'll understand the things that don't seem to make sense to me now, the things that make me scratch my head in bewilderment and sometimes make me want to kick the wall in frustration, or the things that make me fall on my face in grief and sorrow and tears with no explanation for now.

God has promised: *"For now we see in a mirror dimly, but then* [when we get to heaven] *face to face; now I know in part, but then I shall know fully just as I also have been fully known"* (I Corinthians 13:12). I shall know fully just as I also have been fully known! Hold onto that thought. We're coming back to it.

Why not now? Why don't we have all the answers now? The answer to that question may lie in our answer to a few other ones:

What difference would it make to you if you knew all the answers?

How would this change your life?

How would you handle knowing all the answers to your why-questions?

What would you do with the answers?

What would you do with this knowledge?

Would it cause you to love God more?

Would it cause you to love the people around you more and pursue them with great affection and tenderness, longing for a deeper, personal relationship with them, yearning for time alone with each and every single one of them, hoping and wishing for the best possible life for them to the point that you're willing to die for them—not only for the best, but even for the worst of them?

God knows the answers to all our why-questions. And this is what He does with the answers! What would you do?

If you knew all that God knows about the person standing next to you, would you love him or her like this, like God does?

If you knew the reasons why bad things have happened to you and to those you love, would this enable you to never fear or apprehend the future again?

If you knew everything that's going to happen for the rest of your time here on earth, would you be stronger and feel more prepared for what's to come? Or would you be overwhelmed with the weight of it all leaving you paralyzed in inert anxiety, not wanting to face what you see stretching out before you?

You want answers to your why-questions. Could you handle knowing the answers? Are you able?

That's one I can answer for both of us: No. You're not, and I'm not. But God is. That's what makes Him God, and it is in this very essence of His great character of love toward us that He asks us to trust Him with our questions until He sees we are ready for an answer.

I've had a few…answers, that is. Not right away. Not as soon as I asked. But when the answer came, I was satisfied—satisfied in God's deeply personal way of knowing me and understanding my need, not answering until He had prepared me to accept the answer the way He chose to respond. Why? I was left with undeniable evidence that the answer was from Him, and not something I had just fabricated in my own mind!

God prepares us to accept answers to our questions the way He chooses to respond, because then we are left with undeniable evidence that the answer was from Him.

Let me tell you about one of the times God has answered my questions. Some of you have read another book I wrote, *"The Other Side of Silence."* (If you haven't read it, I'd encourage you to do so. You can find it on our website: www.imageministries.com.) In that book, I briefly sketched a picture of the violent, destructive relationship of physical and verbal abuse from my father that my family and I endured. I learned to live with fear every day while I was growing up.

I feared my father. I feared his unpredictable, explosive anger and the beatings that inevitably came with it. I feared the brutal sarcasm and ugly, vulgar cursing that came from his mouth. I feared the instability of never being able to let down my guard completely and enjoy the few good moments of life in those days, always protecting myself from further disappointment, knowing it could all change in an instant of his uncontrollable rage. I feared the feeling of being trapped under the dominion of his control, forcing us to do whatever he said, with no hope of ever escaping the turbulence to find peace—the lasting, quiet, uninterruptible peace for which I longed.

I eventually left home and tasted peace in two new relationships that began to rebuild my heart and refill it with hope that love exists which does not disappoint and does not discourage. I was introduced to "The Gospel of John" in the Bible and met a man named Jesus, though more than a man. Thirty-two years ago, I decided to walk with Him and began a journey that continues today. He has shown me love—spiritual love, Father-God's love to me through Him. I was also introduced to a man named Dominique, though only a man. Thirty years ago, I decided to walk with him and began a journey that continues today. He has shown me love—physical love and emotional love that leads to spiritual love, Father-God's love to me through him.

My parents finally divorced during the first year of our marriage, and Dominique and I rarely saw my father. This seemed fine with both my father and me. My father was finally able to be alone and live the hermitical lifestyle he had always preferred (which family demands had incessantly and frustratingly interrupted, in his view), and I was able to get on with my new life, finally free of the constant struggle to survive the daily onslaught of vulgarity and violence which caused an underlying current of anxiety and stress around my father. God's work rebuilding my heart and refilling it with hope, and the love I was continuing to discover with Dominique, gradually began to encourage me to believe I was getting rid of the awful, nagging fear of my father that had overwhelmed and dominated my life for so many years.

Then one morning while Dominique was at work and I was at home alone with our baby son who was asleep in his crib, I heard a knock at the front door. I looked out an upstairs window and saw that it was my father! Immediately, all the old fear rushed to the surface and my heart was pounding! As he walked around the house and continued to knock on doors and windows calling out my name, I hid, crouched down on the floor of our son's bedroom, filled with terrible fear that if I let him in while Dominique wasn't there to protect me, my father would get angry and turn on me and hit me again! He finally gave up and left.

Relief from this sort of pressure was one of the reasons I enthusiastically agreed with Dominique to move back to live in France with our two small children. At least I wouldn't have to worry about my father unexpectedly showing up on my doorstep anymore! We thought we had moved to France to live there forever. But, as I said before, things don't always work out the way we think they will, do they?

Two years later, after we were resettled in our new home back in the United States, I suddenly told Dominique I felt convicted of my selfishness stemming from the fear of my father and thought it was wrong that he hadn't seen his grandson for over two years and had never even met Fietka, his granddaughter. Dominique agreed that we should make an effort, but he would not allow me to go alone to find my father. He also insisted we would not take the children with us to this first meeting, never being quite sure of what sort of mental or physical state we would find my father. In keeping with his desire to live like a hermit, my father had no telephone, so we would not be able to let him know in advance that he could expect a visit.

Of course, during the 25-mile drive to his house the evening we set out to find him, I rehearsed what I would say when we arrived. We found the trailer park where he was living then; and when he opened his door, he seemed surprisingly glad to see us. We went in and sat down to talk with him (after we moved all the pornographic magazines out of the way), and the small talk gradually opened the way for the reason of our visit.

I said, "Dad, we'd like you to come to our house for dinner on Sunday. You haven't seen Kacha for over two years and you've never even met Fietka. Will you come?"

He never even paused to consider it. He just said, very matter-of-factly, "No, I've seen you and you've seen me. We both know the other is alive, so why don't we just leave it at that."

Swallowing my shock and personal hurt at being so abruptly and unfeelingly shoved aside one more time, I tried hard to guard my composure. I wanted to press on to another question I knew I had come to ask, which was of far more importance than my own request.

"Dad?" I asked quietly. "What about your life? Where are you headed? What about God and Jesus Christ and eternity? What about heaven? Have you changed your mind about that?"

As usual, as it had been my whole life, just the mention of God and Jesus Christ threw him into a rage! He began cursing in anger and jumped up off the couch, coming at me with his arms raised and his fists clenched. Dominique stood up in front of me and managed to calm him down. We left.

I leaned against Dominique as he drove home; and I cried. I couldn't imagine anyone living like that. I couldn't imagine how someone would not want to see his grandchildren. I couldn't imagine how such anger and bitterness could continue so strong in someone's heart.

"How can he live like that?" I asked Dominique.

He didn't. Three months later, he was dead. When I received the telephone call from my older sister telling me that Dad had been found dead in his trailer, I just lifted my face toward the ceiling (toward heaven) and wept. I knew I had been the last one of the family to see Dad alive. I knew I had asked him point-blank whether he had turned to God and put his faith in Jesus Christ. I knew he had not. My sister (and later, the rest of my family) thought my tears and sorrow were because of the relationship I had with my father. They always knew I was his favorite and surely thought I was sorry he was dead. I wasn't sorry. I was glad! I was relieved, finally freed from the fear of his presence in my life and in the lives of my children!

Yet as relieved as I was, I still wept because, for the first time, I was facing the reality that someone I knew personally had died and was probably now in hell for eternity. I wept because as bad as he was, and as much as we may think he deserved what he got for all the hurt and pain he caused the rest of us, it still overwhelmed me with sadness and sorrow and grief to consider the finality of it all. In the assurance of my own faith in God through the work of Jesus Christ, I look forward to someday being in heaven. As far as I know, my father is in hell! I had some vague, storybook notion of what hell is like and how horrible it is. Through the funeral and weeks following Dad's death, I went back to the Bible and searched for a clearer description of it. What I found only brought me to further sorrow and deeper grief.

71

And there was renewed turmoil added to my grief. My uncle was the funeral director who was called to the scene of my father's death and asked to remove the body and prepare it for burial. When I visited his office with my brother and sisters to make arrangements for the funeral, he suggested we skip the viewing that usually precedes the burial. I asked him why. He told us that in his professional opinion, our father had probably been dead for approximately three weeks before he was discovered. He insisted the body had decomposed to a point that we would not like to see. I insisted I wanted to see it. He was shocked and asked me why I would want to do that.

My response was stoic. "I want to make sure it was him. How do you know that wasn't somebody else's body? If it was that decomposed, how can we be sure you really recognized my father? How do I know he's not alive and still walking around somewhere?" My uncle was firm and convinced me I must trust him. He tried to reassure me that he had no doubt this was my father.

I went home that night angry, afraid and upset that I didn't even get the privilege of the closure that death can offer. For weeks after that, my nights were tormented with nightmares of my father coming to our door, or seeing him across the street when I was shopping, or coming around a corner and finding him right in front of me. I didn't tell Dominique or our friends or anyone else in the family, but all the old fears were gripping my heart again as I struggled to ignore the question that haunted my private thoughts, "What if he's still alive? What if that wasn't really him?"

At this same time, our church began a series of evening meetings showing films in which a famous evangelist and teacher shared wonderful stories about his very close, loving relationship with his own father. He was trying to help us see what the love of a father can be like, with the hope of turning our hearts toward God as our Heavenly Father and enabling us to trust a deeper, more personal relationship with Him. But all I heard was what a wonderful father he had while he was growing up, and that only made me angrier!

"Why couldn't I have had a father like that?" I screamed at my friend who followed me into the ladies restroom when I bolted out of the room in the middle of the film one night. She tried to reach out to me and hug me, but I pushed her away and turned toward the wall, covering my face with my hands, angry because of the tears I didn't want to cry and didn't want her to see!

"Don't hug me! Why should *you* hug me? You don't understand! You've had a good father!"

She had no answers, but I had more questions. Why-questions battered my brain and ripped away at my heart, bringing me only further, private turmoil as I grappled with the events of my life that seemed unacceptable—if indeed God had been present then, had known about those things happening to me and my family, and yet had allowed it all and had done nothing to...!

"If God is sovereign and in control over everything in the universe, if He has a plan for each person's life, then why would He allow my father to be born into the family He did?"

"Why would God have allowed my father's real mother to be sick after he was born, never coming home from an institution after his birth, and his father blaming him for the death of his wife?"

"Why wouldn't God have intervened and prevented my grandfather from marrying another woman who was cold, austere and proud and never touched my father while he grew up under her care—never kissed him, never held him, never hugged him? Why couldn't my father have been raised in a family that taught him how to be loved and how to love others?"

"If God is all-powerful, why didn't He ever stop my father from hitting us and beating us? Why did He just let it keep happening, time after time, all those years?"

"If God can change a person's life, why didn't He change my father?"

"Why couldn't my father even die right, the normal way like other fathers do? Why do I have to come from a family whose father was dead and rotting away on the face of the earth for three weeks before anybody knew it because nobody ever saw him and nobody cared?"

"Why can't I even be given the peace of knowing where my father is now? My Christian friends whose fathers have died are looking forward to being together with them again in heaven someday. Maybe my father said a last-minute prayer just before his final dying, gasping breath and turned to the cross asking God to forgive him and receive him. I can't even know for sure if the famous prayer of the thief on the cross saved him or not! Why can't I have some assurance like other Christians do?"

The mental and emotional distress started to have its effect on my body. I lost my appetite, was losing weight, and was having more and more trouble sleeping through the night. I finally decided there must be something wrong with me and went to see our family physician who was also a Christian friend and a member of our church. He examined me and then asked questions about what was going on in my life. Finally he got around to asking if he had heard correctly that my father had recently died. When I told him that was true, he asked me to describe my relationship with my father.

When I finished, he told me there was nothing wrong with me physically, I was simply grieving the loss of my father so much that it was affecting me in physical ways.

"Grieving? You've got to be kidding me!" I exclaimed in total disbelief. "I am NOT grieving! I would be grieving if I had a relationship with my father! I had NO relationship with him!"

The doctor allowed my outburst and then quietly responded, "Yes, you did, Linda. In fact, you had a very strong relationship with him. You had just as strong a relationship with him in the negative sense as some people have with their fathers in the positive sense; and you are grieving just as strongly as those who lose a father they loved dearly."

I found it hard to believe what he was trying to explain to me, but I didn't argue with him. I trusted him and respected him. I simply didn't know what to do with the information he had just opened up before me. It was only information.

Explanation, even graciously given by a trusted friend when we are so deeply troubled and hurt, just explains. It doesn't heal. It doesn't close the wound. It doesn't stop the pain. It only explains why it's all there. It doesn't take the burden off our shoulders or off our hearts. It just reveals the burden so that we understand it more clearly, but we still walk away with the burden. I continued, more quietly perhaps, but I continued to live with my great, private wish for reassurance—for a touch of comfort and a word of peace that would, once and for all, relieve my fears and put my why-questions to rest, letting me get on with life.

Had no one else tried to comfort me? Hadn't a single friend or even my husband tried to reassure me and help me? Yes, of course they had. And I was not ungrateful for the effort that was obviously painful and difficult for each one of them. Why painful and difficult? Because we all know, we have all had the experience that even when we try our hardest to reach out and touch a friend in heartache and pain—to say just the right words to soothe and quiet the heart in our attempts to demonstrate to our friend that we care and that we hurt with him or her—somehow, we know…our efforts fall short. We walk away saying to ourselves, "Why didn't I do this," or "Why didn't I say that?"

Who can touch deep enough to silence the thoughts that plague us?

Who can speak words that are strong enough to pierce the pain?

Who can stop the struggle and take away the fears?

Is there no one here?

Is there no one we can turn to?

Once scarred by the events that leave us with our burden of why-questions, are we meant to continue our journey across the face of this planet, for the rest of this brief one-breath experience called "life," forever strapped with our questions?

Are we expected to simply accept this as destiny, fate, or "my lot in life?"

That summer, our family attended an outdoor Christian music and teaching festival in Virginia, called *Fishnet*. It began on Wednesday and, though most people lived so far away that they had to leave after the Saturday evening celebration, there was an outdoor worship service on Sunday morning offering the rest of us an opportunity to quietly reflect on all we had learned that week. There were probably only about five or six hundred people left by then, spreading across the hillside on our blankets and lawn chairs. As the service was ending, the founder and director of the festival moved to the microphone and said he wanted to pray for us before we left to go home.

But before he started praying, I watched his gaze scan across the crowd in front of him and heard him say, "I believe there are people among us today who are grieving. I'd like us to pray especially for those people. If you are one who is grieving the loss of a loved one or a family member, would you please stand up right where you are and let us pray for you?"

Everything in me rebelled against the urging sense that I should stand! I had no desire to endure a public moment when I knew I could not be sure to control my emotions! The tears I didn't want anyone else to see were always too near the surface. I felt my fists grip the blanket our family was sitting on as the battle of stubbornness raged inside of me.

I don't remember when I actually pushed myself up off the ground and stood on my feet. I glanced around me just long enough to realize the hillside was dotted with other solitary figures also standing. The embarrassment of feeling like I was making a spectacle of myself along with the rest of them forced my head down, my eyes to the ground, squeezed tightly shut in my determination to keep back the tears.

Refusing to look up at him, I heard the director continue his preparation for praying with us. In a gentle, caring voice, he tried to assure us that though the person we knew had died and certainly we would continue being sad because we will miss that person for the rest of our lives, we should also ask God to help us rejoice because now that person is in heaven enjoying the wonderful presence of their Lord and Savior Jesus Christ face-to-face! He urged us to turn from our sorrow and accept the peace God offers as we look forward to the time when we'll be together again in heaven!

My head shot back up again and, in the furious anger I could sense welling up inside of me, I looked around me at the other standing people! It was obvious they were all in agreement with what he was saying, some weeping quietly, others simply nodding their head in silent acceptance. I knew he meant well but, feeling so horribly different and separated from those "good" people in their "good" families, all I wanted to do was obnoxiously raise my hand in the air, interrupt the director's stream of platitudes, and yell, *"Excuse me! Mine's in hell, okay?!"*

Thankfully, my natural shyness prevented me from doing that. Instead, I turned my back on him, stomped off our blanket, and walked until I was a safe distance away from everyone else. I had to distance myself. I knew I had no part in what they were doing and could not endure the power of that disappointment standing in their midst. Standing there alone in my own patch of green field when the director started to pray, I felt my head bow and my eyes close. But I was not praying, not with them. I was wishing again. I was weeping again.

I do not know where she came from. I cannot tell you today what she looked like. I don't think I ever saw her face. I don't think I ever opened my eyes while she was there. But someone came. It was a woman. She never said a word. She just came up in front of me, wrapped her arms around me, and held me. I was too tired to fight. I was too tired to push someone away one more time. I laid my head on her shoulder and wept. It seemed to me, I wept for a long time. She didn't move. She didn't speak. She stood so very, very still and continued to hold me.

Because she was willing to wait, because she was willing to be silent, I finally heard. Because a human being was willing to hold back her own words, I was finally able to hear the words of My Lord. Only a few times in my life have I heard the Lord's voice. This is the only time I have heard His voice weeping. But somehow, it soothed me to hear that the Lord was weeping, as I was. Through that weeping Voice, I heard three things:

"I know your grief, my child."
(Father-God, affirming constant love. I wept. There was silence.)

"All that could have been done was done."
(Holy Spirit, always revealing truth. I wept. There was silence.)

"I, too, weep. I died for him."
(Jesus Christ, taking on the pain. I wept. There was silence.)

I stood for a long time in the silence that followed. I wept until I finally felt my body start to relax. My shoulders slowly dropped, the muscles in my arms relaxed, and my clenched fists gradually opened. When I raised my head and opened my eyes, there was no one there. The woman was gone. I do not know when she left. I looked around quickly, sure that she had just left and I would notice someone walking away from me, wanting to thank her. There was no one near me.

"Was that real? Was there really a woman here holding me?" I wondered, stunned by the power of what I had just experienced! Within seconds, the joy I felt bursting in my heart was so overwhelming that I didn't care! Whatever it was, whoever it was, I was grateful! I didn't know who had held me, but I knew the Voice I had heard!

The words I heard had assured me, finally completely assured me...God knew. God knew me, knew I was hurt, knew I was weeping, knew exactly what I needed to hear: that He had known...

—known my father, known every circumstance of his life, known who he was and sought him, pursued him, called him, offered His love time and time again;

—known me, seen every fight, stood by me in every battle, watched the pain and anger and hurt grow and build its walls around my heart, time and time again calling me, pursuing me, offering His love.

Some people accept what God offers, some don't. I did. To my knowledge, my father didn't. My choice, my father's choice. Should I blame God? No, God did...His part? No—God does everything that can be done in His tremendous love toward us! We humans are just not privy to seeing it all. That's why it's called trust.

I knew the answers to my why-questions had come, not as I expected, but undeniably from God as He chose to respond! Have I had no more why-questions since then? That is not true. There are still some...unanswered. There will always be some, this side of heaven. But, I'm learning to wait. I know that God knows, just as I am fully known!

"Thinking it through"
(Optional Personal Application)

Suggestion: Let's return to the first statement we saw in bold print in this chapter and read it again.

Sometimes bad things happen to good people because good people make bad choices.

Tough to admit, but it's true, isn't it? You may find yourself shaking your head in sadness, even as you read that statement again—old memories (or perhaps recent, newer ones) flashing through your mind, of those you have known and loved becoming tangled in a web of confusion or destruction because of bad choices. The consequences can be devastating and can last a long time, can't they?

But this may be even tougher. Now read the sentence again, this time personalizing it (if you're strong enough to face up to the answers!).

Sometimes bad things happen to me (and the people I love) because I make bad choices.

Suggestion: Some things are coming to mind, aren't they? Are you willing to take some time and write down what you're thinking about? But just to keep things in a positive, constructive light (wanting to help you work further in allowing God to transform you, as we have spoken of in previous chapters), here's how I would suggest you handle each memory:

"God, please forgive me for the time(s) I made the choice(s) to

_____

_____

_____

_____

_____

_____

_____
_____
_____
_____
_____
_____
_____
_____. I recognize now that it was my choice, and it led me into bad consequences. I submit to Your direction, and ask You to wash my mind and my spirit of the terrible guilt I've carried because of my foolishness. Help me to make wise choices that will be in agreement with Your plan to make something new and good in my life from now on."

Suggestion: But other's choices have also made you live through terrible, horrible circumstances that have left you rocked to the core and riddled with unanswered questions. Could personalizing the key principle from this chapter and saying it aloud as a prayer help you? Are you willing to try it?

"God, prepare me to accept answers to my questions the way You choose to respond, because then I will be left with undeniable evidence that the answer was from You."

Chapter 8

When You're Shaken

Oh how God does love us! Oh how I want you to see that God loves you! Oh how God wants you to understand this and accept it, to reach out and take the gift of His love and pull it in toward your chest, to wrap your arms around it and clutch it tightly, squeezing out every bit of its goodness until the sweetness drips down over you, washing and cleansing, moistening the dryness and soothing the burns until you finally relax and allow it to simply rest over your heart and mind and soul!

And what will you find when you finally relax? God's gift of love is who you are! You are God's gift of love! Who He has made you to be is God's gift of love to the world! Who you allow Him to enable you to become is God's gift of love to you!

If we will allow Father-God to repair and rebuild our hearts by committing ourselves to regularly spend time alone with Him, He will begin the wonderful outpourings of blessing from heaven that will refill our hearts. We will meet God again—the One who is Creator and Designer, Revealer and Comforter, Mediator and Savior—this time coming to us as the Strengthener and Restorer. His work in our hearts will strengthen our confidence in who He is, and we will learn to build our hope and rest our assurance on the great and perfect goodness of His character, restoring us from constantly falling into the trap of relying on who we are and of building our hope on any good parts of our own character.

And He will finish His work well. It is promised. *"For I am confident of this one thing, that He who [begins] a good work in you [that is, Father-God] will perfect it until the day of Christ Jesus"* (Philippians 1:6).

As I learn to go out into the world to face my together-times with other people and face the circumstances life brings to me banking on the fact that, since I am God's child, Father-God loves me and will never leave me or abandon me or desert me, I am strengthened. As I learn to trust Father-God to gradually rebuild my heart, I see my character grow and my behavior change, and I am strengthened and restored. As you and I learn to trust God and have faith in His unchanging desire to love, protect, nourish and cherish us, we will be restored to the image He sees in us and restored to trust ourselves to love others—free to let them get close, free to let them touch us, free to be ourselves and no longer worry about or fear what they might be thinking of us or what they might say to us or what they might do to us.

And then you'll finally be perfect? No. You'll make no more mistakes? No. Life will finally be easy; arguments and fighting will stop; and accidents, disease and disasters will finally stop blasting through your door when you least expect it? No. Decisions will be less complicated, dreams will always come true, and everything in life will always have a happy ending? No. Life is still hard, isn't it?

You are a child of God but, for now, you're still living here on earth. This side of heaven, there is still conflict. There are still battles. There is still hurt, pain, sickness, and heartache. There will still be hard, hard times you must live through, and you will be shaken. You will feel buffeted, battered, and bruised, and at times your faith may falter or threaten to fade. The struggles of life—the things men, women, and children do to us, and the stupid, foolish things we sometimes do to ourselves and get ourselves wrapped up in—can drain us and drag us down, can't they?

I know. I've been there, too…drained and dragged down by the struggles of life and the things men and women have done, by the things our children have lived through, by the things I let myself do and get involved in. I've been there, too…shaken! But, my friend, that is why I can stand before you and say, "Oh how God does love us!" The very moment when I was shaken, the One who has the power to be Creator, Designer, Revealer, Comforter, Mediator and Savior was also capable of strengthening and restoring me!

When you are shaken, God is not unaware. He is active. He is not still. The Strengthener and Restorer will orchestrate whatever it takes—don't forget, He can move mountains if He wants to—in order to bring together whatever or whoever is needed to help you stand up again and walk back out into your world with renewed vigor!

God will orchestrate all that is needed, bringing into your life whatever or whoever will help to restore you, so that you may walk again with renewed strength!

I know. I've seen it happen, not only in our own family, but I've also seen God provide help for others in His unmistakable manner of orchestrating life events. The timing leaves no room for doubting His power to move and meet us right where we are in our great need. How do I know? He has moved us to meet someone's need once or twice!

Our move to live in England is one example. Before we moved to England, we were living north of Detroit, Michigan, and belonged to a church where we had invested a couple of years teaching and leading a Sunday School class for young married couples. We were grateful for the opportunity to witness the work of God's Spirit renewing and strengthening the hearts and minds of those young couples just starting out on their journey of faith in marriage together. Our time among them had been so fruitful and rewarding for us all, it was hard to accept God was calling that season to its end and moving us away.

But we obeyed His call and made the final move to our new home south of Birmingham, England, early in the month of December. By January, we had barely finished setting up housekeeping again when an email showed up on our computer screen from a person we had never heard of before. It was from a young woman in Michigan who excused herself for writing without even knowing us, and it was a plea for help. This is what she said:

"Greetings to you from America! Tonight I had dinner with two dear friends of mine, a young married couple who were in your Sunday school class. I was sharing with them about the marital crisis two of my friends in England are experiencing, and that I didn't know how to help them. They told me their teachers had just moved to England, and they gave me your email address. My friend is a young American woman who is married to a British man. They were married two years ago, but now they are both hurting themselves and each other deeply. Oh, and by the way, they live near Birmingham. Any chance you live near there and would be able to see them?"

So, let's make sure we don't miss the details here. A young woman, originally from Indiana, left her roommates and college classes in California to move to England and marry a British man. That couple set up housekeeping north of Birmingham two years before a man, originally from France, and a woman, originally from Pennsylvania, (that would be us!) moved from Michigan to live in England on a temporary job assignment south of Birmingham, arriving there just ONE MONTH before this email-call-for-help was sent out! Do you see the incredible road map laid out before you?

The company my husband works for thought they were the ones sending us on a temporary job assignment. We're convinced this British-American couple was a large part of our true job assignment! And the connections continue. Twenty months after we began counseling that young couple, when I went back to Michigan to be the speaker at a woman's retreat, the young woman who had sent out the original email-call-for-help plus the mother of the American wife in England were both there! I got to meet them personally and, through the teaching I shared that weekend, God granted me the opportunity to be instrumental in their lives, also. What blessed worship we enjoyed together as all three of us recognized God's tremendous love, orchestrating whatever it takes, to help us in our time of need!

My friends, it is no shame to admit when you are shaken! Do it! Go to your church, go to the group of Christians you know and trust, go to a Christian counseling center, or go privately to your Christian brother or sister and cry out, "I'm shaken!" Let them know it! They can help! They may not have answers for you but, at the very least, they will now know how to pray for you more specifically. They may also be among those whom God will use in the plan He is orchestrating to strengthen and restore you.

Why don't we go for help? Why do we hide? Why don't we want other people, especially Christians, to know that our faith is slipping, or that our beliefs are getting jumbled up and confused in our minds, or that our resolve to stand by our declaration to trust in God is weakening? Sometimes it's because we're proud! Our pride gets in the way! We don't want to appear weak to other Christians who seem so strong!

We secretly agonize, "Who will ever trust me again and come to me as a friend to help them after they find out I was shaken?" My friends, show me a Christian who has been shaken but his or her faith remains, and I will show you where wisdom can be found! At his side! At her side! See it through with him, stand by her, struggle it out with him when he is shaken, and treasure her friendship while she is restored, and you will benefit from the great wisdom these people have gained by living through faith that is shaken, but remains!

But if you are the one who is shaken right now, if you're the one who is struggling, if you're the one who is suffering, and you hide…I tell you plainly what a foolish thing you are doing! You can be as godly and righteous as you want to appear to everyone else, and you can tell me you're dealing with this privately because you don't want others to be disappointed or hurt because of what's happening to you…and I'll tell you, you're hiding! As you hide, you're preventing others from learning all the wisdom they can learn from you by going through your experience with you!

You can tell me, "God can just deal with me Himself. He doesn't necessarily need to use others. Besides, if I go to anyone else, then I have to explain all this aloud and dig out all the hurt and pain all over again." And I'll tell you, you're hiding because you're afraid to let them get too close and you're afraid of what they'll think of you. End result? You're blocking all the blessings they can pour over your spirit as they learn to love you, and serve you, and help you when you are shaken!

But, perhaps you have good reasons for hiding. Maybe your reasons for hiding can be lined up right alongside each person in the past who did not strengthen or restore you when you were willing to let it be known that you were shaken. Instead of strengtheners and restorers, did you meet judges?

Other readers have told me it's often very helpful when an author shares a personal story to illustrate a point. It seems to help make the connection between my mind and yours, my life and yours, somehow enabling the reader to accept what has been taught because, "She knows what she's talking about." Perhaps a personal story will help here too.

I have been shaken more than once since I became a Christian more than thirty years ago. There have been events unexpectedly thrust into my life, so brutally disrupting my very existence and causing such violent, emotional reactions, that I have felt rocked to my core! I wish I could say that in every case the assurance of my faith did not weaken or waver as I struggled to maintain daily routines and continue resolutely to serve the ones I love while walking through the horrendous, tumultuous circumstances that suddenly surrounded me. As I said, I wish I could say that. I can't. It is not true. Instead, there have been a few times when my faith has faltered—when I felt God was distant, and wondered why He hadn't intervened, why He hadn't answered, or why He had allowed things to happen the way they did.

My faith faltered on September 11, 2001, and during the week that followed the terrorists' attacks in New York City and Washington, D. C. At that time, we were living in Spain. Our son and daughter-in-law, along with a friend of theirs, had flown to Spain just two days before the attacks expecting to enjoy a two-week vacation with us in our new home near Barcelona.

Did I say, enjoy? It started out that way. The sense of celebration and joy that dominated our first moments of reunion at the airport continued throughout the next two days, as they discovered and reveled in the scenic beauty of the vista from the terrace of our lovely Spanish home situated on a mountain overlooking the Mediterranean Sea. Their initial reactions of pleasure and admiration only heightened everyone's anticipation of discovering the many other beautiful sights we planned to show them while they were with us.

Two days after their arrival, we came back to our house after a gorgeous day together under pristine, blue skies and warm, golden sunshine exploring one of the many Spanish, coastal villages along the Costa Brava. I was cooking dinner for us when the telephone rang. It was a friend from America, calling to make sure we were aware of what was happening in the United States. Not having watched any news yet that day, we had no idea. I ran quickly outside to the terrace where Dominique was sitting peacefully reading a book, told him what I had just learned, and ran back inside to turn on CNN, the only news channel we could receive in English on our television. The television stayed on and we remained there watching it until 2:00 in the morning, when we finally pulled ourselves away from it to go to bed and try to get some sleep.

In many ways, all sense of enjoying a vacation together disappeared the moment we received that first telephone call. In fact, I've told friends since then that it felt as if our time together turned into a "Survivor Show," one of those shows on television with people who are left on a deserted island. The sequels follow the group's efforts to deal with their new circumstances and figure out how to survive! Only to me, it seemed like we became five islands—each one of us intensely struggling to find a way to grapple with the immensity of the destruction in the attacks. At the same time, we knew we must control the fear that threatened to overwhelm us whenever we considered the possibility of further attacks or where future events might lead.

After watching replay upon replay of the planes hitting the twin towers of the World Trade Center in New York City and the fires that erupted after the impact of the planes, knowing there were people in the top floors of both buildings, I was overwhelmed with horror and found it difficult to go back to the kitchen to continue preparing our dinner—something that suddenly appeared so mundane and insignificant.

Then after seeing the huge clouds of dust and debris explode through the streets when those immense towers collapsed and crumbled, people covered with ashes and rushing hopelessly for cover while they desperately sucked for clean air to breathe, and witnessing an unprecedented exodus of the masses of people walking side-by-side across the bridges of Manhattan trying to get out of the city and find safety, I was quaking inside that such destruction and devastation could happen so quickly, so unexpectedly, and be caused by only a handful of men!

This was not an army! There was no formal attack of war by another nation! This was the work of only a few men who had lived and walked among those they intended to kill while they secretly and patiently prepared themselves to fulfill their mission of hate and violence! I was overwhelmed, seeing more clearly than ever how vulnerable we are in the world we must deal with today! I felt my own vulnerability and a sense of the frailty of our human existence, as I never had before! And facing all of this while living overseas as a foreigner only heightened my anxiety.

But, I told no one about my feelings. I was secretly ashamed of myself for reacting like this. I was struggling but didn't want to admit it because as Christians we're supposed to be strong in the face of adversity, aren't we? We're supposed to trust in God through trouble and remember His faithfulness to save us. We sing songs that praise Him for His power to save us and be our strong arm in the face of enemies, right? Right. I've sung those songs, too. And I believe those things about God. But there I was, finding it hard to sleep at night because of violent visions and nightmares, and finding my imagination constantly bombarded during the day with new scenarios of suffering, this time perhaps involving my own family.

We personally knew no one who had been involved in the tragedies in New York City, Washington, and Pennsylvania, though we've heard plenty of stories since then from friends whose family members were there and experienced the trauma firsthand. But our daughter was not with us in Spain when all this happened. She was there in the midst of it all, in America; and we were wondering what would happen next. Would there be more attacks and would she be safe? Our daughter-in-law's family was there too, and we felt helpless, waiting to be assured that they would be all right. I thought of family members and friends we love all across America who we hoped would be safe and protected. If I was able to lay those thoughts aside for just a little while, I only had to look across the room at our son and daughter-in-law there with us in Spain, knowing they would have to board a plane in ten days to fly back to their home in the United States, and my anxieties would rise up again.

Finally, at the end of that first week after the attacks, I could no longer hide my emotions and struggles. After we turned off the television news late that night, I looked at my husband and finally said aloud the thoughts that had constantly been repeating in my mind.

"Honey, can you please help me? I'm having trouble trying to see God in all this. Where was God?"

"Why didn't He stop those men, or reach them with His love so they would change, or turn those planes and prevent them from hitting those buildings? He's all-powerful and Almighty! That's what we believe! But how do you proclaim that now to those people who lost loved ones in this tragedy?"

"I'm in the midst of writing a book about how much God loves people. Who's going to believe that now? How could I possibly look at a person who was watching their television on September 11th and perhaps saw people jumping out the windows of those buildings, knowing their husband, wife, son, or daughter worked on one of those upper floors and wondered if it was their own loved one they were watching jump to their death—and then tell the person that God loves him?"

"In the face of a tragedy of this magnitude, how can we confront people who don't know God, but have experienced this level of trauma and suffering, and expect them to believe us when we tell them about our faith in God? How can we expect them to willingly accept what we're convinced is true when we urge them to believe that He is the Only True God of the universe who is powerful above all, knows everything, loves them and was willing to suffer and die for them so that they could be saved? Would it surprise us if they reacted by asking the same question I'm asking: Where was God on September 11th?"

I didn't tell my husband what else I was thinking. I was seriously considering throwing this manuscript away. I was so distraught, facing the incongruity of the words I had been writing to convince others that God loves them in light of the reality of life at the moment, that I was ready to slice my backup floppy disc in two and give up on the project!

I know the message that God loves us is true, but the timing made it look ridiculous!

The quiet strength of my husband's faith has never disappointed me. He did not disappoint me that night, either. He patiently listened while thoughts, questions, and doubts poured out of me and he allowed me to empty myself. Then he shared a vision that quieted my spirit and shed a small light of hope into the dark turmoil of my confusion. He reminded me of the stories that long ago became our traditional family treasure: *The Chronicles of Narnia*, by C. S. Lewis.

Dominique said when he looked at the towers of the World Trade Center as the planes slammed into them, he imagined seeing the face of the Lion, Aslan (who may depict Jesus Christ in *The Chronicles of Narnia*). He imagined the Lion's huge face filling most of the sky behind the towers and growling with ferocious anger at the evil He saw being acted out in front of Him. But when the towers crumbled and collapsed, Dominique said that, in his mind, the Lion's face would have become full of grief and sadness with tears streaming down from his eyes—so grieved is God, at the tremendous pain and suffering that evil causes. The vision from Dominique's imagination did not completely settle my confusion, but I went to bed with a returning sense of calm in my spirit, and secretly decided that maybe I should wait a little longer before making my final decision about what to do with my unfinished book manuscript.

I didn't have long to wait before God made it clear how mistaken I was to think the message of this book would appear ridiculous if published so close to the events of September 11th. The next day, in the midst of the regular Sunday morning worship service in our church (The International Church of Barcelona), our senior pastor, Mike Chandler, read a quote during his sermon, and a phrase in the middle of it struck my mind. I cannot recall whom he was quoting or what were the rest of the words, but the phrase that struck me was: "...love among the ruins..." I immediately realized this was the key to dispel the rest of my confusion and resolve my struggle about publishing this book! I also sensed I had just discovered the title of the book, as well!

The attacks of September 11, 2001, have left behind huge heaps of twisted, broken, melted steel, broken glass, and pulverized concrete where buildings once stood. Those buildings are ruins now. But the terrorists did more than destroy buildings. Their violent hatred ended life for many, changed life for many more, and altered the course of history for everyone in the world. Whether we want to accept it or not—whether or not we're willing to consider the far-reaching consequences of this event in the realms of world politics, financial structures, international relations, and the global market as the trickle-down effect grows and spreads—the world has changed since September 11th and we will never be the same again.

Why do I say that so forcefully? I say that, because we must now make a decision. We must make a choice that many of us were not confronted with before these attacks. A few men, enlisted, enabled, and encouraged by the organizations that backed them, fulfilled their desire to strike a decisive blow against a nation they have decided is their enemy. Their organization has also made it clear they intend to strike again and continue their campaign to tear down the people and the infidel, capitalist system they hate. What is to be our response, we who have been struck, we who know they could strike again anywhere in the world? Will we now hate, as we have been hated?

It is only natural to look at the ruins of the World Trade Center in New York City, or the crushed-in side of the Pentagon in Washington, D. C., or the debris-littered field in rural Pennsylvania and feel anger, disgust, and revulsion. The desire for retaliation and vengeance may rush to the surface of our emotions. As an initial reaction, it is only natural. But left unchecked, it will soon breed that which is most opposed to the nature of the human beings God has created us to be and wishes us to become. Those responsible for this murderous invasion should indeed be apprehended and brought to justice. But the great danger, once this is accomplished, is that the unchecked bitterness we have permitted to fester and grow in our wounded minds and hearts will, by then, be so deeply imbedded that we will not be able to stop the flow of our anger.

I told you I was shaken and rocked to my core by the magnitude of the pain and suffering we witnessed on September 11th. Though this upset me and forced me to deal with fear and a heightened sense of personal vulnerability, a much greater concern was the apprehension for the future which was growing inside of me while men searched for survivors in the ruins and sifted through the debris for evidence. The news reports of retaliation towards Arabs, or Arab-looking individuals, or Muslims in the United States, and the expressions of hatred toward those who practice the Islamic faith which we have personally witnessed here in western Europe, have revealed the crucial decision I earlier said we must make: We must decide who are our enemies.

Because of an isolated, extremist faction of a few men who say they are Arab Muslims, are we going to choose to hate all Arabs? All Muslims? Will we be filled with hate like the terrorists? We have already seen where such hate leads: the results are catastrophic and irreparable. My friends, I say to you, we must force ourselves to bridle our reactions and control our thoughts as we rebuild our lives! We must seek the ability to find love among the ruins—the ability to trust the Arab-Islamic persons who are our neighbors and offer them the same kindness and humane consideration we ourselves expect from others, separating them from the extremists—or we will be destroyed. But this time it will be far more devastating because, unlike the terrorist attack that came from without, we will be destroyed from within.

Unchecked anger and bitterness in the heart always leaks out and erodes into even our most common relations with others. The poison of bitterness is so lethal it cannot forever be contained and kept bottled up in the human mind. It will eventually burst out and blast its venom on those around us, often when we least expect it and are most assured we have it under control. But our ability to rationalize and justify our behavior, by blaming it on others, restores our sense of personal justice and we continue...perhaps not even realizing that the horizons in our world of human tolerance and acceptability continue to shrink. How small we will become!

But this is not only true about our choices after a terrorist attack. The words you have just read must also be brought into focus when you consider the rest of your life with the wounds and scars you may carry on your heart as a result of those things we've described that others have done or said to you.

After hearing our pastor use the phrase "...love among the ruins," I went home and looked again at a picture of the pile of rubble that was once the World Trade Center. My mind replayed the moments when I had watched those towers crash to the ground, and the analogy suddenly became clear: this is exactly what has happened to so many people! Their lives have crashed and broken, burying them under an incredible weight of complicated consequences! As shocked as we were by the level of destruction in New York City, do we recognize that every day we are surrounded by people whose lives are in a similar state of despair and devastation?

Do you recognize this is true about your own life? To whatever extent you identify with the analogy I just shared—whether it applies to

91

your whole life which is presently in a disastrous state of confusion, or it only applies to a portion of your past that you have never dealt with and you are still wounded with unresolved pain—I urge you to take to heart the strong warning about unhealed anger and bitterness. All, or a portion, of your life was ruined by the words and actions of others. My friend, you must find love among the ruins! You must make the effort, now, to face the issues involved with your wounds! Choose to ignore my warning, and you will not escape! You will someday face your wounds again, but it will be when you realize you have allowed them to slowly destroy you from within!

I am completely convinced there is only one way to escape the slow, lethal poisoning within you. First, you must find God's love. This is why I've written this book and sought to describe Father-God, Jesus Christ, and Holy Spirit to you, hoping you would grasp a clearer understanding of the love God offers you, hoping you would desire to personally experience His love and open your heart completely to His touch.

The past may seem catastrophically damaged and relationships may appear irreparable, like the ruins of the World Trade Center, but I tell you the truth: only God is able to do what is impossible in human terms! Only God can heal you completely, picking up the scattered, broken, fragments strewn like debris around you—like the exceedingly dry bones in Ezekiel's valley of vision—reconnecting disjointed relationships, and rebuilding a life worth living when there doesn't even seem to be a foundation left to build upon. Only God can do such things! But first, you must turn to God.

Next, you must turn away from anger and bitterness and find love that will enable and empower you to live freely among your neighbors, perhaps even near the ones who caused your suffering. And herein lies my final warning. You may now be convinced the anger and bitterness inside of you must be dealt with and you must learn to forgive those who hurt you. Releasing your grip on the grudge you've been carrying against them, you set out determined to behave differently. But even though you realize this, you are still not convinced you need God's help. I tell you, you are wrong. Without God, you will eventually fail and experience anew the terrible proof that you are still tethered to the past—the scars are still there. Only God has the power and authority to break those bonds and heal the scars!

And what will you find when you turn to God? The Strengthener and Restorer will come and orchestrate all that is needed, moving into your life whoever you need to renew your quest for goodness and joy in life. Be willing to reveal when you are weak and admit when you are shaken. Allow others the opportunity to help you, and you will find they are not all judges. Decide to surrender your heart to love God first, above all, more than anyone or anything. Desire His plan for your life and His will in your relationships, and you will discover that God's gift of love to you is...who He enables you to become!

Linda Azema

"Thinking it Through"
(Optional Personal Application)

Suggestion: Sometimes it seems like God is distant or silent. At some time in your life, it may have appeared to you that God did not hear your prayers. In the Bible we can read stories of people who also experienced these things. Find these verses in your Bible and record your reactions to what happened in their lives.

Genesis 30: 1-24 (especially, verse 22)
Can you make a rough estimate of how many years passed between when Rachel begged her husband for a child in verse 1 until God answered her in verse 22? _____

_____

Why do you think God waited? _____
_____
_____

Why do you think God eventually granted Rachel's desire? _____
_____
_____

Can you describe a similar reason why God has waited, or is waiting, to grant your desires or those of someone you love?
_____
_____
_____
_____
_____
_____

In the light of what you are learning about God's character and His love for you, what would you say to express your faith and trust in Him and thank Him for, at times, waiting to answer prayers? _____

_____

_____

_____

_____

_____

_____

_____

John 11: 1-45 (especially, verses 4, 15, 25, and 40)

Why do you think Martha and Mary sent word to Jesus? _____

_____

_____

What was the first thing Martha said to Jesus? _____

_____

What was Mary's first reaction to Jesus? _____

_____

Reread the four highlighted verses again (4, 15, 25, and 40). How did Jesus respond to the situation? How does this contrast to the disciples, Martha, Mary, and others around them? _____

_____

_____

_____

Considering what verse 45 tells us happened at the end of this story, why might God have been silent or waited in your life in the past? _____

_____

_____

_____

_____

_____

_____

_____

God may have allowed suffering and death in your life. Though it is agonizingly hard to live through, such experiences can teach us much about God's love for us. Can you, honestly, tell God how you feel about that? _____

_____

_____

_____

_____

_____

_____

_____

_____

Suggestion: Personalize the KEY principle from this chapter by praying aloud…

God will orchestrate all that is needed, bringing into your life whatever or whoever will help to restore you, so that you may walk again with renewed strength!

Chapter 9

When You Need To Be Reminded

Are you special? Are you valuable? God thinks so, and He wants you to know it! Where did I get that idea? I'll show you. In fact, I'll show you where God's Spirit took me to begin working His thoughts into my mind and through my heart, filling my spirit with prayers for those who will someday read this book or hear this message.

He took me to Isaiah, chapter 62. I experienced a journey of meditation and study in this chapter of the Bible for about six months in preparation for writing this material. When I finished, this simple message was profoundly engraved upon my heart: "I'm special, (so are you). I'm valuable, (so are you). This is God's own high view of me, (and of you also)."

If you have a Bible, you might want to find it and open to Isaiah 62. We'll start at the very beginning in verse 1 and walk our way through the chapter. I'd like to share with you the discoveries I made on my six-month journey into the depths of God's love as He powerfully, undeniably expresses it to us here.

"For Zion's sake I will not keep silent, and for Jerusalem's sake I will not keep quiet..." Let's remember what we've said. Zion and Jerusalem were references to the nation of Israel in the Old Testament. Israel was the nation of God's chosen people. In New Testament times (that means today), all who are Christians are God's people now.

With that thought in mind, I began praying during my meditation times, "Father, for the sake of Your people, for the sake of my brothers and sisters in the Lord, for the sake of Your Church, I will not keep silent. I will speak out! Some may mock me, or ridicule, or walk away, or even try to silence me because they don't like the message. But I will not keep quiet!" Until...what? Look at what it says in the rest of verse 1: *"...until her righteousness goes forth like brightness, and her salvation like a torch that is burning."*

I want to see you shine! I want to see my Christian brothers and sisters marching forward holding high their salvation in front of them, the flame and passion of their faith burning so brightly that the world around them can't help but notice! Notice what? They will notice that which burns brightly is the goodness of their lives (their righteousness)! I want to hear testimony that it is an undeniable reputation for gentleness and love that goes before Christians wherever we go! I want to see us hold forth our salvation, stretching its light out into the darkness surrounding us, firmly gripping the torchlight of truth, allowing it to shine, not in a blinding, obtrusive glare, but in a warm, attractive glow that draws all men to take a second look and come closer to see what this may be.

Who is going to notice when our righteousness and salvation shines so brightly? Just a few people? Only those around us who know us well? Maybe, but look what verse 2 says is possible: *"...and the nations will see your righteousness, and all kings your glory."* Allow your faith to shine brightly like this, make the effort to share the love of God in goodness and gentleness, and everywhere you go people will notice there's something different about you! Everywhere you go among peoples of every nation, even their national leaders will see your salvation because the story of the choices Christians make and how we live (our reputation for righteousness) will go before us!

We can interpret this concept of *the nations* which will see our righteousness in a couple of different ways. First, because of air travel, many of us will be able to visit countries others would never have dreamed of seeing just a few years ago. If we are willing to accept the opportunity this puts before us, we will begin to view ourselves as ambassadors for Jesus Christ in all these places. Since the Holy Spirit resides within us, we take His Presence and the light of Jesus Christ into all these places, even if we're there for only a short visit. By sharing short, small acts and words of righteousness wherever we go, we have the potential to influence lives and demonstrate the love of God to those we meet.

Secondly, because of the transient global society in which we live today, most of us are given frequent opportunities for contact with those from other countries—in our neighborhoods, in our shopping malls, in tourist areas, in schools and universities, in hospitals and medical offices, in our churches, and in the places where we work and earn our living. You and I may never have the opportunity to travel to China as an itinerant preacher and tell the people who live there about the life of Jesus Christ and His sacrifice on the cross. But how many times do we cross the path of a Chinese person in our own country? How many opportunities are we given to allow someone from another nation to see the love of God demonstrated through our words and actions?

Thirdly, there is the issue of *all kings* seeing your glory as mentioned in the promise of this verse. How many of us will ever find ourselves in the presence of a king? Not many, to be sure. But look at this in another way, and we may begin to see there is also opportunity here that we might originally overlook. Let's think of *kings* as those who rule over us. (This fits the normal definition, right?).

If I follow my thought, I can ask myself next, "Who rules over me?" Answer (if I have a job): my boss! Ah yes, you see my point already, don't you? By the choices I make at work, by the manner in which I decide to serve those for whom I work, by the integrity I demonstrate, my boss is able to see my righteousness and my glory—the desire of my heart to first serve God and please Him in all that I do. I have the opportunity to be a living example of the love of God to those around me where I work.

I urge you not to take this lightly. Set your heart toward the desire to please God in such a manner that others will see your righteousness and your glory, and God will not take it lightly, I assure you! But, I say from personal experience, we will never do this perfectly. We will ultimately fail in our attempts to demonstrate God's love to those around us, in fact more often than we'd like. But when God sees a heart that is genuinely seeking to honor Him in this way wherever the person goes, I believe God is pleased to broaden that person's horizons and open contact with more people of different nations than ever imagined!

Growing up on a farm in a little village in Pennsylvania, I would never have imagined I would travel to most of the countries in western Europe, live in France, England, and Spain and learn to speak three languages, giving me the opportunity to spend time among the peoples of those countries. Getting to know the people who live there has given me opportunity after opportunity to demonstrate the love of God that is above and beyond the demands of "the church" they have come to ignore or hate or ridicule because of its history among them! I urge you again: do not take this promise lightly. The nations can see your righteousness and all kings your glory, if you are willing.

Now here comes the rebuilding part. Here comes the personal care of Father-God who met you when you came back to Him and were willing to allow His Son Jesus Christ to unlock the chains that were binding you to your past. Look at the next part of verse 2: *"...and you*

will be called by a new name, which the mouth of the LORD will designate." Why
a new name? Because you're no longer the same person you were
before you came back to God! Because you're no longer living the same
life you were living before you came to find Father-God! Because
Father-God knows you opened your heart to Him and let Him empty it
and repair it!

And Father-God didn't just do all that and then send you away
again! Father-God adopted you! Adopted kids have the right to take
the name their Adopting Father gives them! Quit seeing yourself the
same way you have in the past! You are not the same! The world
around you may not be ready to admit you've changed and may keep on
doing their worst to remind you that you're still the same person. They
will insist that they've known you too long for you to pull the wool over
their eyes. And unfortunately, we may experience this most amongst
our own extended families, but you cannot let them force you into their
mold! God does not see you that way anymore, and He wants you to
stop believing their lies.

"How does God see me?" Have you ever asked yourself that
question personally, just for you—not a bunch of theological, doctrinal
stuff about "Jesus loves me this I know, for the Bible tells me so"?
You've heard that so often, you're not paying attention to it anymore.
You don't even take it seriously. It's just kid's stuff you learned when
you were in Sunday school, or at summer camp, or at Vacation Bible
School. Now you're an adult and I'm asking you to take my hand and
come over here to verse 3 of Isaiah 62 and take a look at God's own
description of how valuable, how precious, and how beautiful you are to
Him!

*"You will also be a crown of beauty in the hand of the LORD, and a royal
diadem in the hand of your God."* Now don't jump up and point to the
words "you will be" in this verse and say to me, "See! It says I will be.
It doesn't say 'you are'!" Right, but work with me here. These words
follow immediately after the ones we read in verse 1 and 2. Those first
two verses describe the wonderful blessings we can enjoy if we are
willing to come back to Father-God and be adopted as His child. The
words we're reading next, starting in verse 3, are only going to happen if
we decide to allow Father-God to touch our hearts. As soon as that
happens, verse 3 begins to describe our wonderful image in our Father's
sight!

Think of it! God sees you as a crown of beauty! So much for my problems about this scar on my face, my crooked teeth and my ears that stick straight out from the side of my head! I have become a crown of beauty in the hand of the Lord! But it gets even more personal. I have become a royal diadem in the hand of...whom? Look at it carefully...in the hand of your God! God has become my God, my Father! I belong! I am not abandoned! I am not deserted!

When I stood in the Tower of London and stared through the thick glass case protecting the crown jewels of the United Kingdom, with armed guards watching every move of every tourist in the room, I had no right to touch the sparkling beauty displayed in front of me. Only a king or queen of the U.K. will ever feel that crown upon their head. Now here is God Himself telling me I no longer need to wonder how it would feel to have that crown on my head. I am the crown! I am the royal diadem, the largest jewel in the center front of the crown!

This is the way God sees me now, and He begins His work so that all the right places will know it. What do I mean? Verse 4: *"It will no longer be said to you, 'Forsaken', nor to your land will it any longer be said 'Desolate'."* God knows you are not forsaken any longer. You belong to Him now. Every angel in heaven knows you belong to God. Your enemy Satan knows you are not forsaken. He and all the demons doing his work know that you belong to God.

Even people around you will start to see the changes in you and in your life. They used to look at you and say, "Forsaken, nothing much to offer, not much worthwhile, not much substance in him or in her!" Not anymore! They used to look at "your land" (that means, your life and everything about you that has anything to do with you—your home, your family, your job, your accomplishments) and say, "Desolate, nothing much to count as a success or an accomplishment or an achievement there!" Not anymore!

Those things will not be said of you anymore. You will not be called Forsaken. You will not be called Desolate. Look at the rest of verse 4 and 5: *"But you will be called 'My delight is in her', and your land 'Married'; for the LORD delights in you, and to Him your land will be married. For as a young man marries a virgin, so your sons will marry you; and as the bridegroom rejoices over the bride, so your God will rejoice over you."* Not forsaken anymore, not desolate anymore because Father-God delights in me! Delights! How pleased does that mean God is with me? How happy does that sound like He is when He looks at me and sees who I am? How much does He love me?

And my land, my life? My life is called "married to God" now! Every time God looks at everything I own, everything I do and everywhere I go, God sees it all belongs to Him! I am His bride and He is celebrating over me! I've given Him everything about me. It's all His, my whole life! But let's remember we're talking about position in life, not necessarily practice. Sometimes God needs to remind me that I am His Bride and, therefore, I shouldn't be doing what I am or using certain possessions in a manner that does not honor Him or please Him.

Talk about repairing my self-image! Talk about emptying out of my heart all the old ideas and critical, distorted images from the world and then refilling it with wondrous descriptions of how God sees me and loves me! How can such wonderful change happen in my life? How could such monumental love possibly break through all the barriers and blockades I had set up around my heart, trying to protect it against any more of the hurt I had already experienced from those in my past who said they loved me?

I'll tell you how. God tells us how. God describes the work that was going on when you didn't even realize it, when you may still have been going your own way, uninterested in or ignorant of the things of God. Verse 6: *"On your walls, O Jerusalem, I have appointed watchmen; all day and all night they will never keep silent."* People were praying for you. I have been praying for you. For all the time it takes me to write a book, every time I sit down to the computer, I'm silently praying for each person who may someday read these words. When we're called by God to pray for others, we don't quit. We don't keep silent. Off and on, all day and all night, the Holy Spirit brings you back into our thoughts and we pray for you.

What are God's instructions to us as we pray for others? *"You who remind the LORD, take no rest for yourselves; and give Him no rest until He establishes and makes Jerusalem a praise in the earth."* God tells us not to stop praying, never to give up. He tells us to keep on begging Him for mercy. We are to give Him no rest from hearing us crying out to Him, pleading on behalf of those we know who suffer, and weeping before Him. We will continue until we see the one we are praying for coming forward to praise God himself or herself, or until we have no more breath to pray! Such is the charge to those who stand in the gap and intercede for others in prayer. Such are those who prayed for you, and this is the reason why you now know such monumental love from God!

Oh yes, you will be rebuilt! Oh yes, you will be refilled! How do I know? I am certain of this because God is the One who swears He will do it, and He is able! Verse 8: *"The LORD has sworn by His right hand and by His strong arm."* The right hand is always referred to in the Bible as the hand of strength, the hand that we use to accomplish the task set before us. The right hand mentioned here is God's own right hand, and it is connected to whose arm? His own arm…which is described how? It is His strong arm. Whose arm could be stronger than God's? Oh yes, my friend. You will be rebuilt. You will be refilled. He is able. He is strong enough, though it may look impossible in human standards.

Nothing is impossible to the right hand of God's strong arm! God is able to repair, rebuild, and refill your heart.

What does God swear will happen when He rebuilds you and refills you by the strength of his strong arm? Verse 8: *"I will never again give your grain as food for your enemies; nor will foreigners drink your new wine, for which you have labored."* God promises to protect you. God promises that all you gain in serving Him will never again be stolen from you. In the past, others have discovered the love, compassion, or mercy in your heart and have come near to take it and help themselves with the goodness you had to offer, selfishly sucking out of you all the benefit they could grab for themselves, and then left you, only to go and parasite someone else.

And now? Verse 9: *"But those who garner it will eat it, and praise the LORD…"* What things will you gain in serving the Lord? A new love, a new compassion, a new mercy that comes from Father-God as He rebuilds in you a new, restored perspective of your life and of other people. This is the "new grain" that you will find and gather into your heart and mind, eating it and digesting it as you recognize this is what truly gives you strength and ability in your daily life.

And why can't this *new grain* be stolen from you? Because the new grain you now count on for nourishment is what feeds your spirit and your soul, the middle of the picture that you had been neglecting and ignoring before! You will want this new food. And where will you garner it or gather it? In the Bible! As you study and learn more, you will eat at the great banquet table God has prepared for each of us there and be fed by Father-God in your alone-times with Him. And thus, you will praise the Lord!

"*...And those who gather it will drink it in the courts of My sanctuary.*" What will you drink? The new wine! Remember what we said the new wine represents when we looked at Joel, chapter 2: the grace of God. You will drink in the grace of God in your alone-times with your Father—His thoughts, His view of life and those you love, His direction and guidance, His strength, His manner of loving and serving, His great joy and peace, patience and kindness, goodness, faithfulness and gentleness.

Where will you drink it? In the courts of God's sanctuary. And what is God's sanctuary now? Your heart! Is your heart being cleansed and repaired and rebuilt so that God Himself now resides there and considers it His sanctuary? If you have chosen to allow God to touch your heart and love you, then yes, my friend, this is the way God sees you!

This is the way Father-God, the great Strengthener and Restorer is at work in you. The distortions the world and Satan had filled your mind with over the years are gradually being cleansed and your focus is being redirected to see yourself, perhaps for the first time in your life, as the Master Creator and Designer originally made you. Your heart has been illuminated by the Light of the Revealer and quieted by the gentle embrace of the Comforter. He is still, and will always be, your Mediator and Savior. For the rest of your life, remind yourself of this often. For the rest of your life, let Him remind you of it.

"Thinking it Through"
(Optional Personal Application)

Suggestion: Whether or not it's new to you, we all need to understand that Father-God adopts as sons and daughters those who place their trust in the finished work of His Son Jesus Christ for their salvation. That's the concept one of the promises of Isaiah 62 gives us: *"...you will be called by a new name, which the mouth of the LORD will designate."*

Why a new name? Because, once you return to Father-God through faith in His Son Jesus Christ—once you make that decision in your life, you're no longer the same person! Father-God has welcomed you into His family and has adopted you as His son or His daughter. Adopted kids have the right to take the new name their Adopting Father gives them! This is God's way of demonstrating that He sees you are now different than you were before. Do you see yourself differently, or are you still allowing the world's view of you to fill your mind?

Suggestion: There are other places in the Bible where God repeats His promise to adopt you and reaffirms His love for you in this way. It may help to read some of them on your own. Look up these verses and record your thoughts and reactions.

John 1:12 _____
_____
_____
_____
_____

Romans 8: 14-16 _____
_____
_____
_____
_____

Galatians 4: 4-6 _____
_____
_____
_____
_____
_____

II Corinthians 6:18 _____
_____
_____
_____
_____
_____

Suggestion: Another promise from Isaiah 62 told us if we set our hearts toward Father-God, genuinely seeking to honor Him wherever we go, then "...the *nations will see your righteousness, and all kings your glory.*" How could that happen in your life? List some of the ways other "nations" could see God's love and goodness (your righteousness) as you go through your daily routine? Who are the "kings" who might see in you God's light (your glory)? _____
_____
_____
_____
_____

Suggestion: Is your heart being repaired and rebuilt as God Himself now resides there and considers it His sanctuary? Repeat aloud the KEY principle of this chapter and ask God to renew the hope and joy of His salvation within you.

Nothing is impossible to the right hand of God's strong arm! God is able to repair, rebuild, and refill my heart.

Chapter 10

When The Best Gift Is Love

I'd like you to imagine that the whole time we've been talking together about how much God loves us, over in the corner of the room there has been a table with gift boxes on it. We would have noticed them there each time we came back into the room together, don't you think? Everybody notices gifts. I'm sure there wouldn't be a single person who came into the room and didn't eventually spot them sitting over there, each one beautifully or handsomely wrapped, obviously ready to be presented to someone. Wouldn't you wonder who they were for or why they were there?

Even though they're all attractive, they're not all alike, are they? Each of us may be able to pick out our favorite just because of personal preference or taste in color or decoration. Imagine one box is decorated in old-fashioned, down-home American country style. Another is done up in contemporary blacks and whites with sleek lines and simple ribbons. Another is covered with gold and glitter with puffy bows and shining Sax Fifth Avenue paper. Another is softer with gentle wildflowers sprinkled over sky-blue paper printed with wispy summer afternoon clouds. And of course, for the male side of our audience we have one that resembles a brand-new tool chest, hard and sturdy with lots of drawers and pockets for stuffing those tools that fit just right in the palm of his hand!

Each one makes a different statement, doesn't it? Your eyes see something different in each one, and you may have a different reaction as you move your view from one to the other. Because you react differently to each of the gift boxes doesn't necessarily mean one box is wrong and another one is right, does it? No, of course not. But because of the way it's packaged, you might immediately be drawn to one of them and secretly respond, "Oh! That one's for me!"

Do you realize we do the same thing with people? When we meet someone or walk into a group or look at a bunch of people across a room as we enter, we can experience an immediate attraction to one person and yet nothing very special about another one. As we get the chance to talk with those same people, for entirely different reasons we can suddenly find ourselves shifting our interest and being pulled over toward another person because of what he says or how she sounds. There can be a certain bubbly fun or quiet caring or depth of life and understanding that attracts me and pulls me toward that person, making me want to get closer, spend more time with him or her and take a look inside.

It's like what we experience when we see the gift boxes. Because of the way they appear, they attract our attention. When you look at these gift boxes, doesn't it make you want to see what's inside? When people look at us, do they want to see what's inside? Uh-oh! Now I'm in dangerous territory again, right? How many of you are sitting there thinking, "Well, there goes your analogy, Linda! You lost me there! I can't exactly follow through with that picture by putting me in it! Sorry honey, but have you taken a good look at me? I'm not exactly what you'd call a gorgeous gift box!"

Ah! Now, there's where you're wrong, my friend. You've got a problem, and that's why you can't follow me with this analogy. What's your problem? You're saying you can't imagine others agreeing that when they look at you, they see you like this: a gorgeous gift! Maybe not. You may be right. When other people look at you, they might not see that. But that isn't what these boxes are meant to picture. When you look at these gift boxes, you're meant to realize this is the way God sees you. Every time God looks at you, He sees a gorgeous, beautiful gift He has created for the world to benefit from and to enjoy!

Look at these boxes again! Look at these gifts! Why do some of you have such difficulty seeing yourself like this—so beautiful, so unique, so precious, so attractive, so valuable? What's keeping you from accepting the fact that God sees you like this and values you this highly? I'll tell you what the problem is. I'll tell you what's blocking your view. I can tell you what's distorting the picture. It's what's inside! What do you still have inside of you, deep down in your heart and mind in those private places you don't let anybody know about, that is constantly at work affecting how you see yourself, and therefore, how you think others see you, too?

What's inside? Well, let's use our analogy of these gift boxes to help us see what that might be. Imagine I go over to the table in the corner, pick up a box, turn around toward you and take the lid off. What's inside this one? I pull out the contents one item at a time: a nice little bouquet of fresh flowers, a few pieces of beautiful jewelry, a soft pair of real leather gloves. But down in the bottom, hidden in a corner of the box, I find a little bag of garbage! Putrid, smelly, leftover trash hidden away in the midst of all that quality and freshness!

What a surprise! Sure did look nice at first, didn't it? But, yuck! Get a little closer and find out what's been hidden on the inside under all the pretty trimmings and, well, it's suddenly not very attractive anymore, is it? Weren't you disappointed? Here you thought you had found somebody really nice. But once you started to get to know her—once you started to get to know him...I wonder if this is why some people can't seem to keep friends, or why some marriages end up fizzling out?

Okay, well let's try this one. I reach over and pick up the second gift box. Taking off the lid, I pull out a lettermen's jacket, an old football, a cheerleader's sweater and a pom-pom. "Oh great!" we think to ourselves. "Here she goes again, talking about when she was a cheerleader in high school, and then the prom queen, and then the homecoming queen in college!" Or every time you spend free time together, he eventually gets around to bragging about how he was once the star of the football team. Don't they have anything going on in their lives today? He's forty years old now and she's thirty-five! Seems like they don't like life today, so they live in the past!

But maybe this one will be better. I take another box and peek inside. Okay, you want to see too, so I pull out a bunch of books, some framed diplomas, letters of recommendation, and a recently updated career resume. The career woman and the market-driven success man! These are their credentials. She's convinced once you know about all these things she's accomplished, you'll be even more interested in getting to know her and hearing what she has to say. These trophies are his ticket into every conversation and the stamp of approval that allows him to hold his head up high among the elite of his field and enables her to feel comfortable and unthreatened when she's out here among the rest of us. Those initials after his name on the program guarantee everyone's interest and attention when he stands up to speak. And to her, the titles of the books she's had published, especially the ones that won literary prizes, are undeniable proof of the value she contributes to the world.

By now, you can see where I'm going with the analogy of these gift boxes, can't you?

The first one worked hard to hang flowers and jewelry and prettiness on the outside, hoping it would cover up the leftover trash and garbage that she keeps tucking back in the corners of her life because she doesn't want to deal with it yet.

The second one is still hoping the same sparkle and flash that got him his letterman jacket or got her the homecoming queen crown will win your approval as well.

And this last one is banking all his hopes on the tremendous respect he'll get from you once you know how smart and successful he is.

Why do we think we have to do all of these things? The answer? What have we been talking about throughout our time together? We do these things because of how we see ourselves, because the view we have of ourselves never seems to measure up to what we think others will expect or want or find acceptable. So we dress it up! So we cover it up! So we build ourselves up!

Don't misunderstand me. There's nothing wrong with flowers and jewelry and gloves and…well, there is something wrong with leftover trash! But there's nothing wrong with sharing your memories that you were a star athlete or a cheerleader or the queen-for-a-day. And there's nothing wrong with diplomas and successful careers and accomplishments. There's nothing wrong with any of those things…unless we use them the wrong way! What's the wrong way? It's wrong when we depend on those things for our sense of personal identity and for gaining approval from others!

Why? Concentrating on those things and depending on those things distracts us, and everyone around us, from seeing the middle of the picture, the real you! Depending on those things and being content with who those things say that I am prevents me from ever coming to Father-God. When I depend on those things, I don't need to rely on God! Talking about myself all the time, working hard to present and promote myself all the time, prevents me from noticing when Father-God wants my attention and prevents me from hearing when He seeks to tell me how He sees me!

Take all those things away (and you watch me push aside all those other boxes we've opened), and ask Father-God what He sees when He looks at you. (I lift up one more box from the pile and take off the lid, saying…) "Here is how Father-God sees you." (I lift only one thing out of this box. You lean forward to see what it is. It's only a mirror.)

Go to Father-God and ask Him to reveal Himself to you. Seek to know and understand and love Him as the One who is Creator and Designer, Revealer and Comforter, Mediator and Savior, Strengthener and Restorer, and He will use His Word in the Bible to show you who you are in His sight. He will hold up the mirror of His Word before you and take the scales off your eyes allowing you to see yourself more clearly than you ever have before.

Simple, isn't it? Not much in this beautiful gift box. Just a mirror. You look inside, and all you see is you. That is exactly what God wants, my friend. He wants you to give Him your heart, allowing Him to repair it, and rebuild it, and refill it with His great love for you. Once God has emptied out the rest of the things I have allowed to clutter up my gift box (my self, the gift God has made me to be), He wants to refill my heart with words from His heart that describe how much He values me, how precious I am to Him, how He treasures me and loves me.

Maybe you've never heard some of the words in the Bible that God has recorded to tell us how He loves us. Maybe you have. But have you ever heard those words and seen your own face in front of you at the same time? Have you ever seen your own face and realized, "That's me God is talking to! That's the way God sees me!"

I invite you to have that experience now. As you read these words, listen with your heart to the message that is from Father-God Himself. These words from the Bible are His Words. He wrote this love-letter to you and to me. Imagine as you read them that a mirror is being held in front of you (or you might even find a mirror and stand in front of it as you read these words aloud.) Look in the mirror and picture this is what God says when He sees your face. You don't even have to be touching the mirror. Just let God's words touch you.

"You are a garden spring, a well of fresh water, and streams flowing...a garden breathing out fragrance...its spices being wafted abroad" (Song of Solomon 4:15,16).

"[You are] my beloved, and [My] desire is for you" (Song of Solomon 7:10).

"I have been the LORD your God...for there is no savior besides Me. I cared for you in [your] wilderness..." (Hosea 13:4,5).

"For [you] are [My] workmanship, created in Christ Jesus to do good works which [I] prepared in advance for [you] to do" (Ephesians 2:10).

111

"I have loved [you] and given [you] eternal comfort and good hope by grace…[to] comfort and strengthen your heart in every good work and word" (II Thessalonians 2:16).

"[You] are as the stones of a crown, sparkling in [My] land" (Zechariah 9:16).

"Don't you know that you are [My] temple and that [My] Spirit lives in you? You are of Christ, and Christ is of God" (I Corinthians 3:16,23).

"You are as beautiful as Tirzah…as lovely as Jerusalem…as awesome as an army with banners" (Song of Solomon 6:4).

"You are precious in My sight…you are honored and I love you" (Isaiah 43:4).

"You are holy…the redeemed of the LORD…Sought out, a city not forsaken" (Isaiah 62:12).

"For [I] created [your] inmost being; [I] knit [you] together in [your] mother's womb…[you] are fearfully and wonderfully made…" (Psalm 139:13-14).

"To you it has been granted to know the mysteries of the kingdom of heaven…" (Matthew 13:11).

"[You] are protected by the power of God through faith for a salvation ready to be revealed in the last time" (I Peter 1:5).

"Truly, truly, I say to you, that you will weep and lament…you will be sorrowful, but your sorrow will be turned to you…I will see you again, and your heart will rejoice…no one takes your joy from you." (John 16:20,22).

"[I] have searched [you] and [I] know you. [I] know when [you] sit and when [you] rise; [I] perceive [your] thoughts from afar. [I] discern [your] going out and [your] lying down; [I] am familiar with all [your] ways. [I] hem you in, behind and before; [I] have laid [My] hand upon [you]" (Psalm 139:1-3,5).

"I…betroth you to Me forever; yes, I…betroth you to Me in righteousness and in justice, in lovingkindness and in compassion, and I…betroth you to Me in faithfulness…[and] you…know the LORD" (Hosea 2:19,20).

"Your light will break out like the dawn, and your recovery will speedily spring forth; and your righteousness will go before you..." (Isaiah 58:8).

"[Your] frame was not hidden from [Me] when [you] were made in the secret place; when [you] were woven together in the depths of the earth, [My] eyes saw [your] unformed body. All the days ordained for [you] were written in [My] book before one of them came to be" (Psalm 139:15-16).

"[You are]...as a living stone...choice and precious in the sight of God" (I Peter 2:4).

"I have inscribed you on the palms of My hands; your walls are continually before Me" (Isaiah 49:16).

"Are not two sparrows sold for a cent? And yet not one of them will fall to the ground apart from your Father. But the very hairs of your head are all numbered. Therefore, do not fear; you are of more value [to Me] than many sparrows" (Matthew 10:29-31).

"[My] love [is] manifested in [you], that [I] sent [My] only begotten Son into the world so that [you] might live through Him. In this is love, not that [you] loved [Me], but that [I] loved [you] and sent [My] Son to be the propitiation for [your] sins" (I John 4:9,10).

"What comeliness and beauty [are yours]! You are altogether beautiful...And there is no blemish in you" (Zechariah 9:17, Song of Solomon 4:7).

"How great is the love that [I] have lavished on [you], that [you are] called [My] child! And that is what [you] are" (I John 3:1).

"[I have] been [your] defense [when you were] helpless. [Your] defense [when you were] needy in [your] distress, a refuge from the storm, a shade from the heat" (Isaiah 25:4).

"You [are] a crown of beauty in the hand of the LORD, and a royal diadem in the hand of your God" (Isaiah 62:3).

"It will no longer be said to you, 'Forsaken,' nor to your land will it any longer be said, 'Desolate.' But you will be called 'My delight is in her,' and your land, 'Married.' For the LORD delights in you, and to Him your land will be married" (Isaiah 62:4).

"I have loved you with an everlasting love; therefore I have drawn you with lovingkindness...I will build you, and you shall be rebuilt...again you shall take up your tambourine...and go forth to the dances of the merrymakers" (Jeremiah 31:3,4).

"Therefore let it be known to you...that through [Jesus Christ] forgiveness [for your] sins is proclaimed to you, and through Him [you] who believe [are] freed from all things, from which you could not be freed through the Law of Moses" (Acts 13:38.39).

"No longer do I call you slave; for the slave does not know what his master is doing; but I have called you [My friend], for all things that I have heard from My Father I [make] known to you" (John 15:15).

"[You are] like a lily among thorns...my darling among the maidens...like an apple tree among the trees of the forest..." (Song of Solomon 2:2,3).

"[You are] a garden locked...my sister...my bride...a rock-garden locked, a spring sealed up" (Song of Solomon 4:12).

"[You are] like a tree firmly planted by streams of water, which yields its fruit in its season, and its leaf does not wither..." (Psalm 1:3).

"[When your enemies] confronted you in the day of [your] calamity, [I] was your stay. [I] brought [you] forth also into a broad place; [I] rescued [you], because I [delight in you]" (Psalm 18:19).

"You are the light of the world. A city set on a hill cannot be hidden. Let your light shine before men in such a way that they may see your good works, and glorify your Father who is in heaven" (Matthew 5:14,16).

"You are [chosen], a royal [priest or priestess],...holy..., a [person of] God's own possession, that you may proclaim the excellencies of Him who has called you out of darkness and into His marvelous light" (I Peter 2:9).

"[I] will rise upon you, and [My] glory will appear upon you. And nations will come to your light, and kings to the brightness of your rising…and you will see and be radiant, and your heart will thrill and rejoice." (Isaiah 60:2,3,5).

"[You are My] vineyard of wine…I the LORD am [your] keeper; I water it every moment, lest any one damage it, I guard [you] night and day" (Isaiah 27:2,3).

"[You] will bear good news of the praises of the LORD. [You] will go up with acceptance on My altar, and…shall glorify My glorious house" (Isaiah 60:6,7).

"…You have been forsaken and hated…[but] I will make you an everlasting pride, a joy from generation to generation…instead of bronze I will bring gold, instead of iron I will bring silver, instead of wood, bronze, instead of stones, iron…I will make peace your administrators and righteousness your overseers" (Isaiah 60:15,17).

"I go to prepare a place for you…I will come again, and receive you to Myself; that where I am, there you may be also" (John 14:3).

"Arise, and stand on your feet; for this purpose I…appoint you…a witness not only to the things which you have seen, but also to the things in which I will appear to you…so that you may turn [others] from darkness to light and from the dominion of Satan to God, in order that they may receive forgiveness of sins and an inheritance among those who have been sanctified by faith in Me" (Acts 26:16,18).

If you were willing to allow those words to touch you—if you are willing to bring your face and your heart regularly before God's Word—you will be changed. Your view of yourself will change. You will see yourself differently and people around you will recognize something different about you.

Look back to Isaiah 62 again. We didn't finish that chapter. In verses 11 and 12, what does it say you will be called? *"Holy, the redeemed of the LORD, sought out, a city not forsaken."* Why will you be sought out? Why will people begin looking for you and coming to you when they are in need of counsel or encouragement? There are two reasons why this will happen:

1) They will recognize that God has sought you out.
2) They will recognize that you have sought God out!

115

You will be known as one who knows the great joy and benefit of seeking God, and of meeting Father-God!

Well, my friend, you have heard the truth. If you had not read this book, if you had not heard this message, perhaps you would not have the responsibility that now lies before you. Of what responsibility do I speak? Simply this:

One who hears what is true must then decide what he or she is going to do about it. Do nothing, and it is worse than if you had not heard.

What will you do with what has been impressed upon your heart and mind? Do nothing, and it is worse than if you had not heard. The Bible puts it this way:

"But prove yourselves doers of the word, and not merely hearers who delude themselves. For if any one is a hearer of the word and not a doer, he is like a man who looks at his natural face in a mirror; for once he has looked at himself and gone away, he has immediately forgotten what kind of person he was. But one who looks intently at the perfect law, the law of liberty and abides by it, not having become a forgetful hearer but an effectual doer, this man shall be blessed in what he does" (James 1:22-25).

What will you do?

What are you going to do with this great message of God's love in which He highly views and values each one of us?

Take it to people all around you! Share this message with everyone you know, even with those who already seem to be firmly grounded in a solid, healthy view of their personal worth before God. Even these stronger ones often need encouraging reminders of God's great love toward them. And certainly, none of us need struggle long to find the battle-worn and broken-hearted who are crying out in their own lonely corners, "Does anybody love me?"—waiting and wishing for someone like you to come and offer hope and reassurance.

Isaiah 62, verse 10 exhorts us: *"Go through, go through the gates!"* Pray your way through the barriers people have set up to keep others from touching them! Ask God to show you how to break down their walls!

"Clear the way for the people!" Ask God to make it plain to you how to clear the path in front of the confused ones around you so that they can see their way to Father-God. But when you've asked God to make it plain to you, and He answers plainly, then follow His instructions. Obey

what He tells you to do, even when it's tough love He asks you to demonstrate.

"Build up, build up the highway!" Let God direct you in mapping out a strong, sure road to God, pointing out the signposts and indicating the signals God is using to draw each person to Himself. And yes, you can be specific! At times, we must be specific in order to overcome the tremendous human capacity for justifying and rationalizing our own behavior. There are times when the person we are praying for is allowed too much room to squeeze around the generalities we share. It becomes necessary for us to find the courage to point directly at the problems.

"Remove the stones!" Pray and ask the Holy Spirit to reveal to you what could be blocking a person's way toward accepting God's love. What is she stumbling over? What keeps tripping him up? God will show you. Then have the gentle courage to take your friend by the hand and walk with him or her directly over to the *stone* God has pointed out, and offer to bend your knees together in prayer and help remove it out of the path.

"Lift up a standard over the peoples!" You have seen me do this throughout our time together. The standard of God's Word—God's view of us, Father-God's love for us, and the call to His choices for us—has been lifted up before you. Go and do the same. Leave this place and, everywhere you go, pray constantly for wisdom and discernment, "Holy Spirit, remind me of what is true. Help me sift through the smoke screens and hurtful distortions the world is using to confuse us. When I see these evil things, give me courage to lift up Your standard, Your view, Your love!"

With power, but gentle care—with piercing truth, but tender mercy—with a tenacious grip on God's right hand of promise, but holding out the other hand to help your friend stand back up on his or her feet—speak the truth, and God will be pleased with the gift. He delights in you!

Hear the promises of the One who loves you.

The great...

      Creator-Designer,
      Revealer-Comforter,
      Mediator-Savior,
      Strengthener-Restorer
          says this to you.

I will bring you into your own land.
> You will be restored and returned
> to the place I had planned for you.
I will sprinkle clean water on you,
> *and you will be clean,*
> > as you have never felt clean before!

I will cleanse you from all your filthiness,
> all that the past has heaped upon you,
and from your idols,
> those things standing between you and Me.

I will give you a new heart,
> *and put a new spirit within you.*
I will remove the heart of stone…
> *and give you a heart of flesh!*
> > You will allow yourself to feel,
> > as you have longed to,
> > yet were not freed of your fears!

I will put My Spirit within you
> in a new way,
and cause you to walk
> steadfastly and with confidence
in My statutes…

I will save you from all your uncleanness;
> *and I will call for the grain,*
> > the heavenly food that nourishes the spirit,
and multiply it…
> > You will feed upon
> > and understand My Word
> > with clear sight.
> > > The fog will lift!

I will multiply the fruit of the tree,
> *and the produce of the field,*
> > for you will be truly productive
> > in the work of My Kingdom;

that you may not receive again the disgrace
of famine among the nations,
>   and you will no longer feel
>   like a second-rate Christian,
>   wondering if you could ever measure up!

I will cause the cities to be inhabited,
>   there will be people pouring into your life,
>   as I send them to receive
>   the blessings I am now free
>   to flow through you;
and the waste places will be rebuilt,
>   those places of your life that you thought
>   you had ruined forever with your sin.

Watch Me build something wonderful from them!

The desolate land
>   of your life
will be cultivated instead of being a desolation
in the sight of everyone who passes *by.*
And they will say,
>   *"This desolate land,*
>   this woman we know,
>   *has become* as beautiful as
>   *the Garden of Eden…*
What was *waste, desolate, and ruined…*
>   *is now fortified and inhabited,*
>   REBUILT!

Then all who are…round about you will know
>   *that I, the LORD*
>   *have rebuilt the ruined places*
>   *and planted that which was desolate;*
I, the LORD, have spoken…AND WILL DO IT!"
>   (Ezekiel 36: 24-36, emphasis mine)

119

"Thinking it Through"
(Optional Personal Application)

Suggestion: Read through this list of KEY principles we discovered in this book.

Chapter 1: **God is not unaware of the damage other people can do to us. He knows every detail of the damage that has been done to you.**

Chapter 2: **God is not only aware of how the world has affected you. He also has an agenda for how He wants to help you and heal your damaged heart.**

Chapter 3: **God cannot do (in your heart) what you do not give Him permission to do, because God WON'T do what you do not WANT Him to do.**

Chapter 4: **All of our lives, the world and Satan have been feeding into our minds the very thoughts that stand in the way of simple, childlike trust in God as our Heavenly Father tenderly caring for us in every circumstance and yearning with deep, sweet love to carry us and keep us through it all!**

Chapter 5: **God can take that which was lifeless and dead, and make it come back to life, with NEW life!**

Chapter 6: **The things God has in store to share with me in alone-times with Him are meant to prepare me for the together-times with others which He knows are coming.**

Chapter 7: **God prepares us to accept answers to our questions the way He chooses to respond, because then we are left with undeniable evidence that the answer was from Him.**

Chapter 8: **God will orchestrate all that is needed, bringing into your life whatever or whoever will help to restore you, so that you may walk again with renewed strength!**

Chapter 9: **Nothing is impossible to the right hand of God's strong arm! God is able to repair, rebuild, and refill your heart.**

Chapter 10: **One who hears what is true must then decide what he or she is going to do about it. Do nothing, and it is worse than if you had not heard.**

Suggestion: Pick one principle that seems particularly important to you today, especially in light of circumstances you may be facing at the moment. Write the principle you have chosen: _____
_____
_____

Suggestion: Reword this principle, in your own words, to describe how it impacts the situation you are facing (or have faced in the past). Be specific! _____
_____
_____
_____

Suggestion: What do you think God is asking you to do because of the understanding you have gained by rewording this principle? _____
_____
_____
_____
_____
_____

Suggestion: Reread the warning of the last principle, the one from chapter 10. **"One who hears what is true must then decide what he or she is going to do about it. Do nothing, and it is worse than if you had not heard."** Now compare that thought to these verses. How do you react to what you read?

2 Peter 2: 21 _____

_____
_____
_____
_____

John 9: 41 _____

_____
_____
_____

James 4: 17 _____

_____
_____
_____

Final Suggestion: What do you sense God's Spirit urging you to do as a result of reading this book? Are there changes you should make? Write those things here and finish with a prayer of surrender and commitment to obey God and follow the path He is revealing: _____

_____
_____
_____
_____
_____
_____
_____
_____

(We invite you to share your thoughts, reactions or questions with us. You can email the author at www.imageministries.com)

About the Author

The cross-cultural experience of an American living in France, England, and Spain—along with extensive travel for work and teaching throughout the rest of Europe—has permitted Linda to see life from a fresh perspective. The insight gained has added unusual personal depth to her skills as a communicator and teacher.

The demands for public speaking and teaching seminars on marriage, finance, parenting, and work ethics from a Christian perspective led Linda and her husband Dominique to found "Image Ministries." From a past involving drugs, sexual immorality, and physical and mental abuse, Linda shares hope that lifts barriers to help others find strength to live, courage to love, and the return of quiet joy in the process.

Printed in the United States
26642LVS00005B/262-312